REVELATIONS OF TIME & SPACE, HISTORY AND GOD

Dr. Stewart A. Swerdlow

Expansions Publishing Company, Inc.
Saint Joseph, Michigan
USA

Copyright © 2020 Expansions Publishing Company, Inc.

Published by:	Expansions Publishing Company, Inc.
P.O. Box 12
Saint Joseph, Michigan 49085 USA
269-519-8036
Skype: eventsatexpansions
customersupport@expansions.com
www.expansions.com

ISBN: 978-1-7343408-4-6

Cover Photo by Jonathan J. Swerdlow
www.jonathanswerdlow.com

All rights reserved. Printed in the United States of America. No parts of this book may be used or reproduced in any manner whatsoever without written permission except in the case of brief quotations embodied in critical articles and reviews.

After so many years of writing books and dedications, I struggled to think of to whom or what I should dedicate this book, the third in a series of deeply spiritual and historical information. I have stated my gratitude to my family and supporters in other volumes. I am so glad to be able to research in all corners of the world and bring this often hidden information to the public.

Therefore, I dedicate this book to

God-Mind and The Absolute.

It has given me this mission to disclose vast secrets about existence, history, and even myself. All is One.

We are all a reflection of each other and we are all a thought in the energy of Ain Sof.

What more can you want!

Blessings to all who read this work. I am blessed by all of you.

Books by Stewart A. Swerdlow & Janet Diane Mourglia-Swerdlow

13-Cubed: Case Studies in Mind-Control & Programming

13-Cubed Squared: More Case Studies in Mind-Control & Programming

1099 Daily Affirmations for Self-Change

Alternative Medical Apocrypha: Body-Mind Correlations

Blue Blood, True Blood: Conflict & Creation

Decoding Your Life: An Experiential Course in Self-Reintegration

Healer's Handbook: A Journey Into Hyperspace

Healing Archetypes and Symbols

Heights of Deprogramming

Heights of Health

Heights of Spirituality

Hyperspace Helper

Hyperspace Plus

King Bee, Queen Bee

Little Fluffs Series for Children

Montauk: Alien Connection

Revelations of Time & Space, History and God

Stewart Says…

Template of God-Mind

True Reality of Sexuality

True World History: Humanity's Saga

White Owl Legends: An Archetypal Story of Creation

Table of Contents

Introduction 7
Section 1 11
   Time & Space 13
Section 2 59
   Simbatyon 61
   Hebrew DNA Flow 65
   Africa 73
   Jews of Africa 77
   Rome/Latins 81
   Asia 89
   Miscellaneous Historical Facts 95
   The Sicarii 101
   More Templar History Revealed 111
   Vikings/Hebrews 117
Section 3 129
   God 131
   Kabbalistic Laws and Rules 135
   The Bahir 151
   The Thomas Code/Gospel of Thomas 157
   Secret Plan To Build The Third Temple of Solomon 179
   The Revelation of The Messiah 183
   Koshering of Humanity 187
   Writings of Ari 189
   The Teachings That Cannot Be Taught 193

Appendices 195
   72 Names of God 196
   72 Vortices 198
   72 Names of God with Functions 202
   Names for God 203
   The 72 Living Divine Names of the Most High Instructions .. 204
   Names of 72 Angels Correlated to 72 Names of God 206
   Hebrew Alphabet Chart 207
   Hebrew Letter Correlation to Astrology and Sephirot 208
   Hebrew Letters From Star of David 209
   Ancient & Mystical Alphabets 210
   Glossary 211
   Index 216

Introduction

This volume is the third in a series that includes *King Bee, Queen Bee* and *The Template of God-Mind*. To get the most from this book, I highly recommend you read the other two first and in the above order.

This series is based on many years of study, travel, research, and deprogramming. The books are based on my notes from the Expansions September Spectacular classes and our January Oversoul Extravaganza classes of the last several years.

Those who have attended these classes have found them to be intense, mind-expanding, and even shocking. Participants learned that they do not know what they think they know. Lives have been changed for the better, permanently.

Because there are almost 8 billion people in the world and most of them are not able to attend our classes in Michigan, I have undertaken to present the information of those classes in the best manner possible for those who wish to know truth and become what God and Absolute intended them to be.

Of course, as in most of my work, I take great risk in the reactions of the public. You can imagine that many times, people are not very kind. However, if one is to promote truth and honesty, then bravery and courage are necessary in the face of adversity.

I come from a long line of very independent thinkers, on both sides of my family. On my father's side of the family, my great-uncle, Yakov Sverdlov, was the first President of the Soviet Union. His son, my cousin Andrei, started the KGB. My grandmother was a Soviet spy in WWII.

My mother's family has roots in the old Austrian-Hungarian Empire. My mother's paternal lineage was Romanian, but emigrated to Romania from Poland in the 1800s. There is actually a town in Southern Poland with my mother's maiden name—Jankowicz.

My mother's mother grew up in the Southern Polish town of Rzeszow. Her father, my great-grandfather, was a red-haired, blue-eyed rabbi who was a devotee of the Gaon of Vilna who taught hidden Kaballah and Zohar in the late 1700s. The story of the Gaon of Vilna is outlined in the books of Rabbi Joel Bakst, a scholar in Kaballah and Zohar information.

Many years ago, a researcher in New York City sent me a lengthy genealogy of my Sverdlov family. I went through this report in great detail. I have already written about my family beginning in Thon, Switzerland in 80 AD, and then migrating to Sweden where they became part of the Rus Vikings before invading Eastern Europe and creating the Russian Empire.

But, shockingly, I saw a section in the report that stated a female Sverdlov married into the Bakst family decades ago! A connection to Kaballah and Zohar had been made!

The Sverdlov family spread to Iceland, Greenland, Belarus, France, South Africa, Siberia, Japan, and Australia, in addition to the USA and Israel. But there is more....

In a video I did in Havana, Cuba in 2018, I revealed that one of my ancestors was the 9th Knight Templar that explored the underground area of King Solomon's stables in Jerusalem. That person has never been revealed until now. Like the others, he was a descendent of the Dragon Riders, who became the Pharaoh's guardians and Therapeuts, then went on to morph into the Essenes, Viking Priests, Cistercians, and finally, Templars. His name was blocked from history because he was a Jew. That was unacceptable to the Church leaders.

This is a main reason my ancestors, who travelled with Mary Magdalene to the South of France, then to what is now Switzerland, and then to Sweden to become the push for the Rus. "Rus" means "Rose." This was a reference to the Magdalene. The Templars took a vow to always protect her progeny until eternity.

It is no surprise then, that I married Janet Diane Mourglia, whose family name is directly connected to Mt. Moriah in Jerusalem, and directly descended from Mary Magdalene! Janet is also descended from the Duke of Savoy, who was hidden in safety in Waldensian territory in the Alps. Janet is also descended from Black Saracens from Morocco, and from Cherokee royalty. She is also a great-granddaughter of a Bouvier and cousin to Jacqueline Bouvier Kennedy.

Therefore, these works come to you through time and space and history, under the direction of God-Mind and Absolute. It has been inside of me since birth, waiting for the time in this century when all can finally be revealed. It is a great relief for me and an unloading of a huge task and burden, to present these three volumes, especially this one that you hold in your hands.

Blessings to you who read and understand. Blessings to you who do not. We are all ONE. I offer you my life's work, with all my heart and soul. Thank you.

Section 1
Time & Space

Time & Space

In Actuality, there is no Time & Space. Time & Space are illusions of a linear timeline. Outside of all physical realities, there is only timelessness and simultaneous existences.

Time & Space are measures or markers to give perspective in life, helping you to be aware of events, sequences, locations, and movements.

Movements can be related to the clock, seasons, actions, growth, or aging. Movement is how living Beings determine the progress of life in this reality.

The "Tzimtzum" from the Absolute, explained in more detail in *The Template of God-Mind*, is when the disorganized energies of the Absolute created a space within Itself in order to generate Creation. Tzimtzum cannot truly be demonstrated graphically, but for the purposes of discussion Tzimtzum can be depicted as a circle with a line drawn halfway through:

The line is the phallic symbol and the circle is the vaginal symbol. This, then, became the basis for sexual intercourse. However, at the end of this line, a cube was created that represents the spreading out in all directions of this inserted energy from Absolute.

The cube represents the fractalization/fracturing of energies into all Creation and Existence. The cube also symbolizes the God-Mind as an aspect or attribute of the Absolute. As it proceeded into creation, the cube produced cubes within cubes.

The concept of this cube is outlined in the Kabballah's *Sepher Yetzira*, which means "The Book of Creation." The following ideas, descriptions, further help you understand the concept.

Wikipedia:

The **Cube of Space** is an occult concept that was popularized by the prominent occultist Paul Foster Case. The Cube of Space associates the three axes of the cube, the center point of the cube, the six sides of the cube, and the twelve edges of the cube, with the 22 letters of the Hebrew alphabet. The Cube of Space is based upon two verses in the proto-kabbala text called the Sepher Yetzirah. One of those verses is in chapter 4 and the other verse is in chapter 5. The verse in chapter 4 associates 6 Hebrew letters with six cardinal directions (up, down, east, west, north, south). The verse in chapter 5 associates 12 Hebrew letters with either 12 diagonal directional 'arms' or 12 diagonal boundaries (different translations contradict each other), which some interpret as referring to the 12 edges of an octahedron, though Paul Foster Case interpreted these as the 12 edges of a cube. In the most authoritative English translation of the Sepher Yetzirah, scholar Aryeh Kaplan interprets this verse (Chapter 5, Verse 2) as describing a cube. (Sefer Yetzirah Page 203) While occult author Kevin Townley explains a cosmology with an octahedron within a cube.

From Golden Dawn:

It is in the Philosophus grade of the Hermetic Order of the Golden Dawn, 4=7, that another concept is identified that is classical Qabalah. It is called the Cube of Space. Essentially, the Cube of Space is a road map to the Universe. Ancient Qabalists used the Cube of Space as a glyph or diagram for understanding the nature of the Universe in-depth. It also relates to the Neophyte and Zelator initiation where the Double Cubical Altar is utilized as one of the prime symbols of the Temple. We remember the axiom of the Emerald Tablet that states "As above, so below," or in other words, the Cube of Space is manifested on several levels, both Microcosmic and Macrocosmic. The Cube of Space is referred to in depth in an ancient Qabalistic document called the Sepher Yetzirah. It is here that a direction is assigned to each letter of the mystical Hebrew alphabet. It is in studying the diagram included in this lesson on the Cube of Space and developing an understanding of it that this particular glyph or symbol can be used to demonstrate the extent of which the Qabalistic symbols are meant to help us direct and understand the internal learning process. Please sit down now and try the following meditation. Close your eyes. Think of one thought. As you think of this one thought, ask yourself, "Where does this thought originate?" The thought that you should think about in this particular exercise is the word "I." As you think of the word "I," think in terms of where "I" originates, "What is 'I?'," "Who is 'I?'," "How does 'I' manifest?" Try this meditation before reading on, even if you spend only five minutes with it. Now that you have focused on the internal point "I," you can begin to contemplate and digest your thoughts as to how "I" relates to the principles of the inner Universe. If you think about it long enough,

I'm sure that you'll conclude that these principles are in fact the corners and directions of the Cube of Space. It is like imagining that our consciousness is enclosed or encapsulated inside a cube. This helps give our intelligence something more foundational, something more concrete, though artificial in nature, with which to begin inner self-exploration and inner growth. The Cube of Space is similar in some ways, although very different in many, to the symbolism that we have learned thus far in studying the Qabalistic Tree of Life. In some ways the Sepher Yetzirah describes and helps us understand the Cube of Space with great precision. In another sense though, it does not easily relate this Cube of Space to the Qabalistic Tree of Life. Perhaps one reason for this is that the document, the Sepher Yetzirah, does not specifically describe the paths between the sephiroth as they are understood by modern Hermetic Qabalists. Much of this work was done by S.L. MacGregor Mathers and the Golden Dawn. This work continues on today in the Hermetic Order of the Golden Dawn, giving us a much more indepth understanding of the nature of the Universe. Much of this information will be shared with you as you approach the Veil of the Portal and enter into the Second Order. Many Qabalistic scholars look at the differences between the Qabalistic Tree of Life and the Cube of Space as expounded upon in the Sepher Yetzirah, and they see that what really happened here is an attempt to infuse two conceptually different methods or approaches to the inner planes, using a type of logic similar in some ways to Pythagoras. It is very difficult for some to make an accommodation of the symbolism of the Cube of Space into their modern symbolic structure, but I think that as you examine 72 it more closely, you will find that it definitely has a place in the symbolic understanding of inner planes.

The Cube of Space allows us to look at the Universe from a different perspective than the more accepted Tree of Life. Here is an example of one of those symbolic exortations: Notice on the diagram, of the last page that the Universe card, the letter t, is crossing the three Mother letters at the point of the Universe. This is a very important piece of symbolism because it exemplifies the fact that through the Mother letters of a, m and c, we have final manifestation brought into relationship through the path of t, which is also called the Universe card. In other ways, the Cube of Space is more consistent with some of the traditional concepts of ritual work, such as east, west, north, and south. A significant amount of understanding and meditation should be applied to the Cube of Space. We are not requesting that you memorize where each Hebrew letter or each Tarot card appears on the Cube of Space, but only that you try to understand the nature of the Cube of Space. It can only be understood through innerplane work. It is really a symbol that is beyond physical description with the utilization of words. Until such time as you experience the energies directly and how they cross other energies in your personal working, the Cube of Space will be nothing more than a Qabalistic concept that seems vague at best. Let us remember that all of our symbols in some way or another are artificial, from the Tree of Life, to artificial devices such as gematria and temurah.

Cube of Space: Metapsychology: The Experience of Being Alive

Sepher Yetsira Index

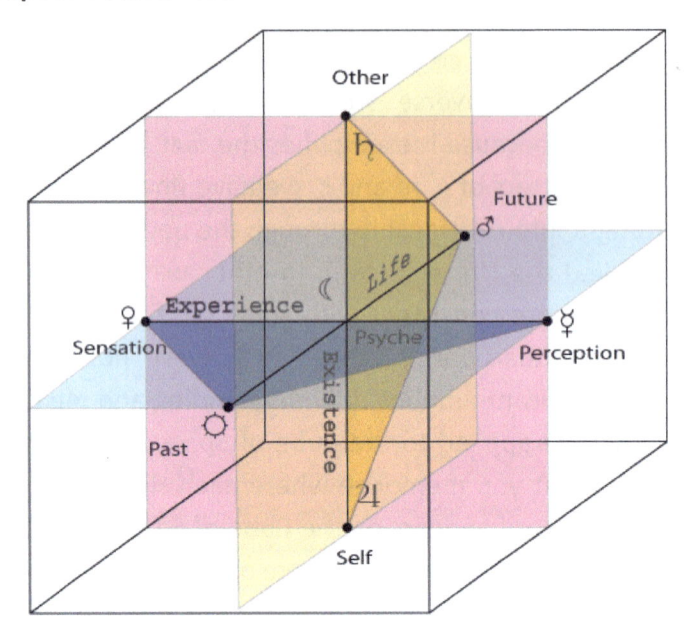

The Metapsychology of the Cube of Space: The Dimensions of Consciousness & the Structure of Human Experience

Abstract: Recent research has begun to explore cognitive domains on the basis of categories such as spatial metaphors, and bodily experience, while the hard problem of consciousness studies is defined as the explanation of subjective experience or qualia (*).

The Cube of Space is a multi-dimensional model of psychological space and an integrated framework for the metaphors of embodied and situated experience. The directions of the Cube are psycho-spatial and symbolic and represent centers or spheres of emotional consciousness which leave their imprint on our neurology, our cognitive processing, our symbolic thought and expression, and our experience.

Metapsychologically, the Cube is a description of "the underlying conditions of possibility for the formation and existence of human reality as it's experienced by the psyche" modeled in 3-D virtual psychological reality.

Linguistic evidence of psycho-spatial orientation and symbolic directions:

Obey your superiors, stand on your rights; face the future, put the past behind you. Don't be left, do the right thing. Center yourself. Kiss up, kick down; look forward, don't look back. Sinister implications, right away. Look inside. Held in high esteem, an object of low regard. Face uncertainty, let the past take care of itself. The devil's on your left shoulder, an angel's on your right. The still voice inside. Lofty ideals, basic instincts; sailing into uncertain waters, back in the old days. Feminine left, masculine right. Inner space. Higher power, lower self; you've got your life in front of you, time's running out, don't get left behind. Left is weak, right is strong. In the middle, at the center, where it all comes together.

Summary: The meaning of the Cube of Space is lost if it is not understood as a description of our own psychological reality. The space in the Cube of Space is our own psychological space and its dimensions are the psychological dimensions of our own experience. We can easily find its "common-sense" descriptions in our own experience and verify their accuracy or usefulness for ourselves.

The Cube of Space describes the human reality of Adam Qadmon, archetypal man, as composed of an inner life formed in the first four Sephirot (spheres of consciousness/

energy) and the axes and center of the Cube, and an outer life formed by the last six Sephirot and the opposing faces of the Cube. The inner life is timeless and the outer life is experiential and developmental.

Inner space, or the interior space of human consciousness, is formed by three primary energies, represented by the Hebrew "Mother" letters: Aleph, maximum energy/consciousness, Mem, minimum energy/consciousness, and Sheen/Seen, the energy mediating between them. Outer space or being is the reflection of those energies as existence, life and experience. Existence is formed by the polarity of self and body/other, life by the polarity of future and past, and experience by the polarity of feeling and thought, or stimulus and response. The psyche itself, the seventh direction of the Cube, is at the center, through which all the energies pass.

Symbolically, our ex-is-tence is defined by self and other, or inner energy and its outer body, with our spiritual goals above and our material development below, and our standing in society. Our life is defined by the uncertain future we face before us, and our past by the actions we have performed and put behind us. The experience of life in existence is made possible by the unconscious impressions of sensuous reality entering our receptive left hand (right-brain) and being met by the cognitive response and action of the right hand (left-brain) Again, in the center is the psyche, the eye of the needle and gateway to our Soul.

This is the view of Adam Qadmon, realized Man. The view of most of humanity is the reverse, as we turn our backs on the future and unconsciously relive the past, while confusing thoughts and feelings and material and spiritual goals.

Looking into Ourselves: the Metaphor of Psychological Space

How do we know where we are going, if we don't know where we are?

We have seen that there are spatial metaphors, neurologically mapped and linguistically programmed. But what of the metaphor of psychological space itself? What is it a metaphor for? Where is the space? And what are its metaphorical dimensions and symbolic qualities?

On the deepest level, psychological space is a contradiction which fuses the two opposites of mind and matter: physical 3-D space and non-physical mental functioning and subjective experience. What could be spatial about psychology and what could be psychological about space?

The Cube of Space is a psychological map that requires us to think psychologically and symbolically about the organization of our own experience in order to be able to read it and find the space it maps. We can use the model of the hypercube, a projection of a 4-dimensional cube into 3-dimensional reality, as a starting point for thinking about the "dimensions" of psychological space.

The Cube is a 10-dimensional model for the totality of human experience and possibility. Our experience of those dimensions, in both material and psychological reality, is a 3-dimensional projection of a higher-dimensional structure existing within and beyond space-time, which is the structure of our own multi-dimensional consciousness.

The Cube of Space maps the intersection of a multi-dimensional structure with 3-dimensional consciousness. What appears as an element of the Cube in psychological 3-space is the imprint of a higher dimension in the total structure. The directions of the Cube are psycho-spatial:

they are symbolic and qualitatively as well as spatially organized, (for example: up-other, down-self, front-future, back-past, left-sensation, right-perception, center-psyche) and its categories are experiential (existence, life, experience).

We can look at the structure and organization of the psychological space of the Cube from the inside-out, starting with the two basic categories of inner and outer space.

Entering Symbolic Space

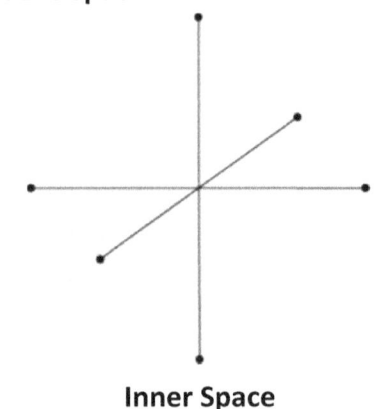

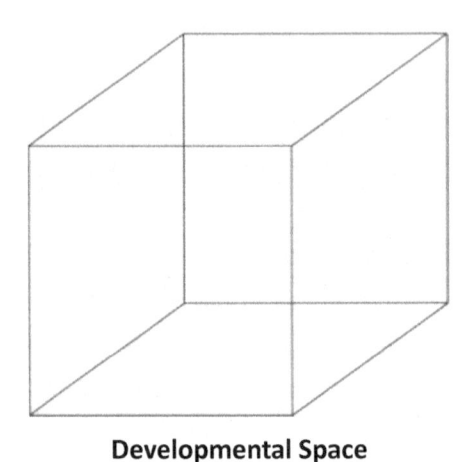

Inner Space

Developmental Space

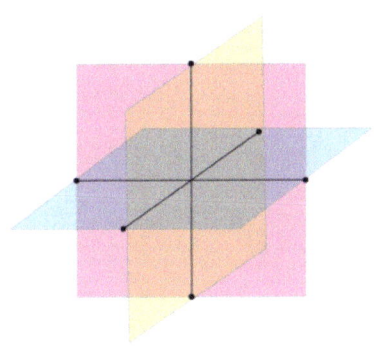

Inner Planes

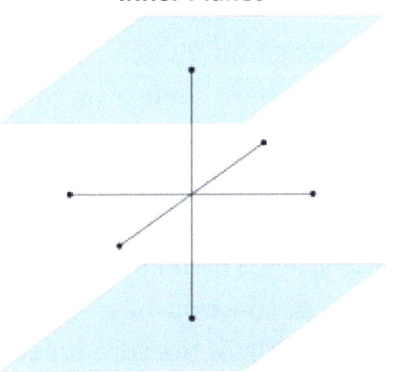

Existential Faces

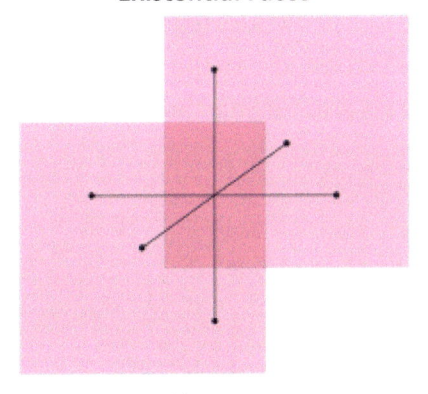

Life Faces

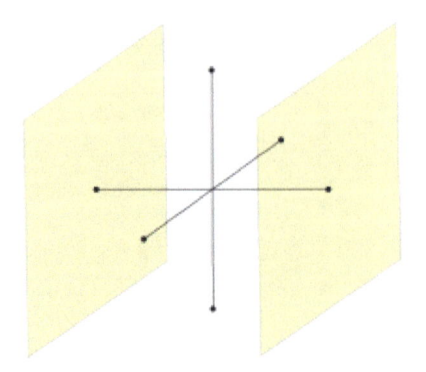

Experience Faces

It is difficult to begin to visualize psychological space, though most feel they have some awareness or subjective consciousness of an "inner" experience. The Cube differentiates psychological space into an inner, non-developmental (no)space and an outer, experiential and developmental space. Inner inner space is defined by the core processes of the materialization of consciousness; outer inner space is defined by the expansion of the core processes into experiential space where psychological development can take place. The three basic axes/categories of existence, life and experience are extended into the six opposing faces of self-other, future-past and feeling-thought.

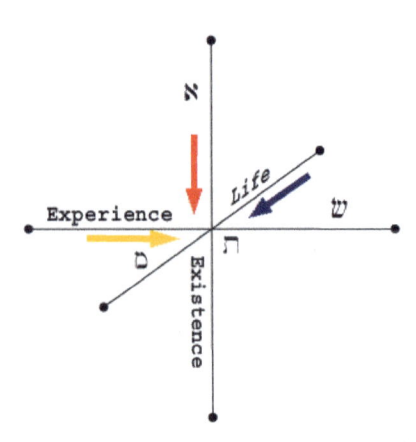

The axes define flows of energy: from top to bottom, from front to back, and from left to right, symbolizing a flow from spirit to matter, from future to past, and from sensation to perception.

Each of the twenty-two structural elements of the Cube -- center, 3 axes, 6 outer directions, 12 edges -- is specified by one of the twenty-two letters of the Hebrew alphabet, representing a "semantic prime" or "fundamental power" of creation.

The initial transformations of energy in the first four Sephirot defining Adam Qadmon's inner life and space are driven by the three Mother letters Aleph, Mem and Sheen. These letters, plus Tav, formative of the Psyche, complete archetypal man's true interior space, beyond the developmental dimensions of the last six Sephirot. Together, they form the Ten Sephirot Belimah of the Sepher Yetsira.

When projected or extended into the outer dimensions, Aleph, archetypal maximum energy/consciousness, completely beyond space-time, becomes its opposite, Yod, existence in duration. Mem, existential minimum energy/consciousness is the matrix for life, Hay. Cosmic Sheen, their interaction, becomes union (Waw) or experience of life in existence.

The axes differentiate into polarities in psychological developmental space as the faces of the Cube. That means that opposing faces are related as two aspects of the fundamental energy of their axis. Existence differentiates into self and body, life into future and past, experience into feeling-thought.

The Cube of Space as described by the Sepher Yetsira is a complex, multi-dimensional, multi-layered, abstract object. All its categories are related and semantically linked across multiple levels of description, and we will use only a few of them in our outline of psychological space. The most basic categories of the Cube are the letters of the Hebrew alphabet (autiot) and the numbers of the Sephirot (spheres of consciousness/structuration). In the outer dimensions of psychological-developmental space, we find the multiple, layered specifications of sephirot, formative letter, planet and contrary quality. We will have the opportunity to see how all these levels are related and integrated in our expansion of outer psychological space, beginning with the Sephirot.

Because we are going to use a few symbols drawn from the symbolic languages of the Hebrew alphabet and ancient astrology, see Astrological Equations in the Sepher Yetsira if you are unfamiliar with the planetary symbols and the alphabet of basic "formative operators" referenced above for more background. In any case, behind each symbol, letter or number, is a precise description of its underlying energy and inner meaning and its relationship to other symbols. We will develop our outline of metapsychological space by adding layers of symbols and descriptions which are actually equations that need to be solved and integrated within oneself. Where else would you find a precise description of your own inner psychological space?

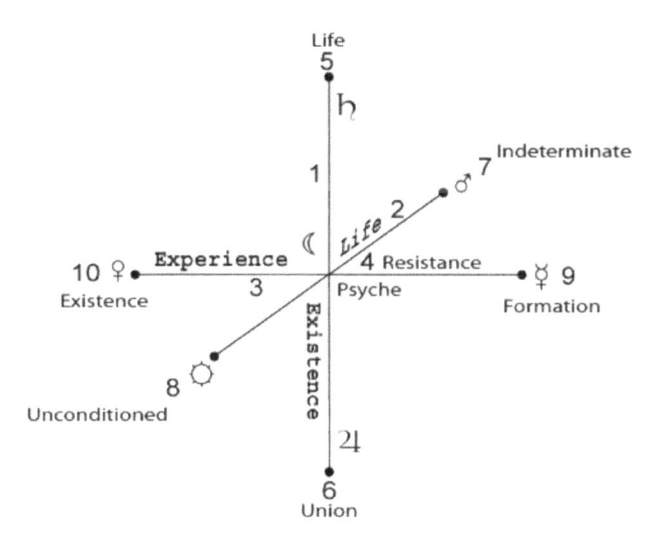

```
                    Life
                     5
                     •
                     ℎ
                                        Indeterminate
                  1              ♂ 7
                         Life 2
  10 ♀  Experience  《 ┌─────────┐    ☿ 9
  •─────────────3──┤ 4 Resistance├────•
  Existence         │   Psyche   │   Formation
                    ╞════════════╡
                    │Existence   │
                  8 ☉            │
                  •              │
                Unconditioned    │
                                ♃
                                 6
                               Union
```

The numbers of the Sephirot define the most basic structural aspects of the dimensions of the Cube. We can use the basic formative meanings of the numbers to build our first structural level and gain insight into how the dimensions are psychologically defined and logically and common-sensically organized. The first outer sepherot after the interior first four is 5=Hay/Life. The sixth is its opposite, 6=Waw/Union, defining the existential axis. These are the most generalized descriptions of the sepherot, underlying formative letter, planet, contrary-quality and other levels of qualification.

We might ask: what are the most basic qualities of the basic categories of human reality? Psychologically, what is the deepest level of meaning of existence, life and experience, and their projections as body, self, future, past, feeling and thought?

The Cube says that the existential axis is defined by a flow from life (of the body) to union (self); that the life axis is defined by a flow from the indeterminate, uncertain (future) to the unconscious, unconditioned (past); and experience is defined as a flow from existence (sensuous reality) to formation (perception/thought).

Next, we add the Hebrew formative letter associated with the Sephirot.

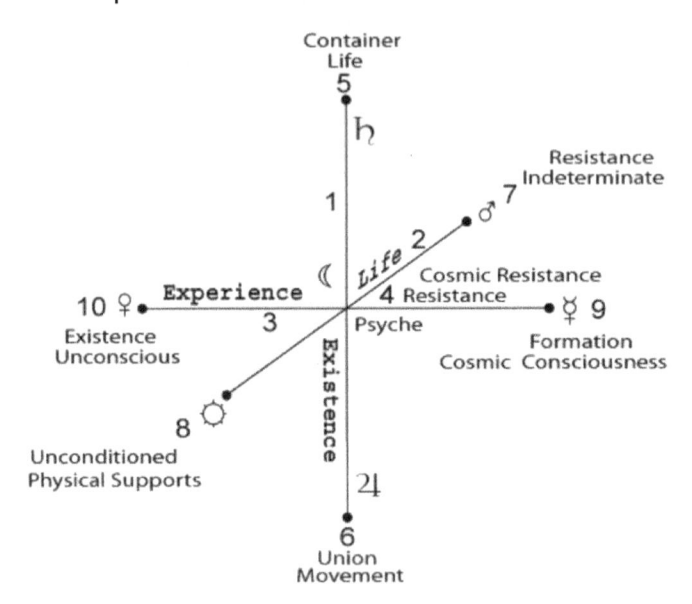

When a question is raised whether a scientific term is a sign or not, there will be no doubt that the word representing the term is one. Whatever a quasar or quark really is, the words "quasar" and "quark" are undoubtedly signs, created artificially to designate esotermic phenomena. But what happens if someone postulates that the enormous energy emitted from a quasar erupts from the word "quasar" itself? What if a scientific system arrives at the conclusion that the mountain emerges from the word "volcano"? In such a case, it will be possible to surmise that the word is the signified, while the material representation is the sign. This is actually the system presented by the *Sepher Yetsira:*

The letter of the alphabet is the source of the planet, and not a sign by which it is designated.

The Language of Creation and Its Grammar
Joseph Dan, *Jewish Mysticism, Vol I*, Aronson, 1998, p.151

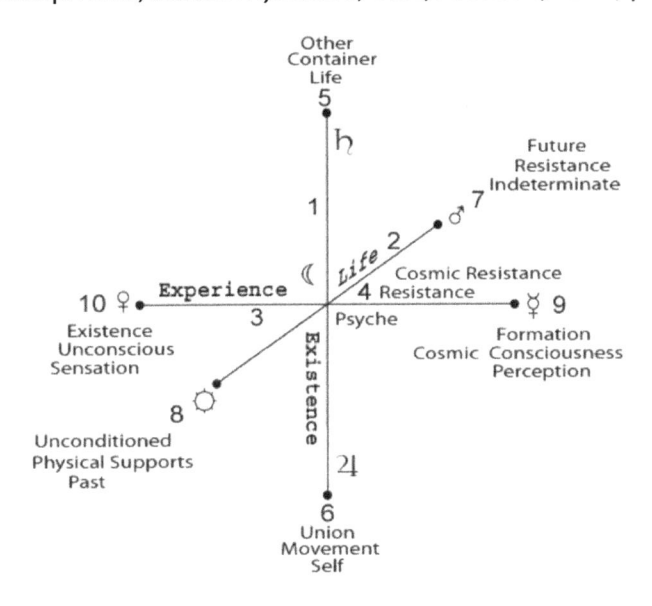

```
                    Other
                    Container
                    Life
                      5
                      ♄
                                    Future
                                    Resistance
                   1              Indeterminate
                                7
                           2  ♂
                        life
              ((        Cosmic Resistance
    Experience         4 Resistance
10 ♀                                    ☿ 9
   Existence    3    Psyche
   Unconscious       ᴱ            Formation
   Sensation         ˣ        Cosmic Consciousness
                     ⁱ            Perception
              8 ☉    ˢ
                     ᵗ
   Unconditioned     ᵉ
   Physical Supports ⁿ
   Past              ᶜ
                     ᵉ
                            ♃
                      6
                    Union
                    Movement
                    Self
```

The formative letter ("the source of the planet") adds another level of categories which relate to the first two (axes and sephirot), and further differentiates and characterizes them. Psycho-spatially, up/other is a container for life and down/self is a union of inner movement; we resist the indeterminate future in front of us and structure it with what we turn our back on (repetitive unconscious actions); our feeling of what's happening is mostly unconscious and the formations of our thoughts have their roots in cosmic consciousness or universal mind.

As our metapsychological model unfolds, we can see better how the fundamental categories are logically related. Existence is composed of self-other relationships (starting with the body). Life is the course of psychological development ("the maturity we have not yet attained") determined by our future conflicts and our past actions. The experience of human reality -- life in existence -- is made possible by sense-perception.

The primary categories of reality are psychologically dimensionalized and spatially organized. In the universe of psychological space, they are symbolized by the astrological planets, which differentiate the inner flows of the three axes into the six outer centers of consciousness/energy.

As with all our formative "translations," the terms that we have been rendering as the psychological categories of self-other, future-past and sense-perception (as well as psyche) are all defined by specific equations in the meta-structure of the Cube. We will use one example to show how the Cube defines our psychological future with the equation for the planet Mars.

What is the future, psychologically? The Cube defines it on multiple levels: as indeterminate and unpredictable and the source of real possibility (Sephirot number); as our resistance to the possibilities of own development through the repetition of unconscious actions (the psychological past) (formative letter). The next step is the energy of the planet, which is "formed" by the Hebrew letter, and which in turn forms the six faces plus the center of the psychological Cube of Space.

"Mars" as an arbitrary linguistic symbol tells us nothing about the qualities of the abstract energy it refers to, except as it points to a mythological reference (Aries (Greek) or Mars (Roman) as the God of War). As we shall see, the mythological associations of conflict and war are derivatives (shadows, really) of the meaning of the true "god" behind the word.

The sephirotic number and formative letter are simple, one letter designations. The Hebrew words for the planets are complex multi-letter "equations" for the energies they refer to, and exist in a hierarchy or matrix of related equations. Beside being logically and meaningfully related to each other, the planets are related upward to the formative and sephirot, and downward or outward to their own (contrary) qualities and their signs and formatives.

Multi-dimensional abstract objects have multi-layered and interconnected levels of meaning. We'll scratch the surface with the multiple layers of meaning of Meadim, the Hebrew word for the planet Mars.

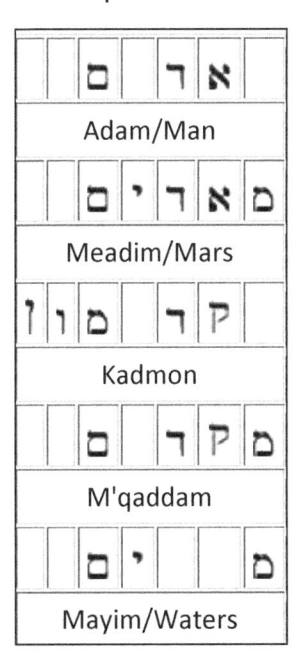

ם	ד	א

Adam/Man

ם	י	ד	א	מ

Meadim/Mars

ן	ו	מ	ד	ק

Kadmon

ם	ד	ק	מ

M'qaddam

ם	י	מ

Mayim/Waters

Meadim, the equation for Mars, the psychological quality in front of us, is spelled Mem-Aleph-Dallet-Yod-Mem. The equation for archetypal man, Adam, is spelled Aleph-Dallet-Mem. Mayim, the sea or waters, is spelled Mem-Yod-Mem. The direction East is spelled Qof-Dallet-Mem.

Meadim is then defined as timeless Adam (itself Aleph in Dallet-Mem, blood) in the symbolic waters of existence or duration (Mayim). All of the directions are described by similarly complex planetary equations. But in only one does Adam Qadmon see himself in a state of resistance and conflict between the spiritual Aleph and the material Yod (Meadim). At still another level, M'Qaddam, The "East," or symbolic future of Adam is Adam himself with cosmic Aleph, Qof (Cosmic Consciousness) substituted for Aleph: Qof-Dallet-Mem instead of Aleph-Dallet-Mem.

Because the flows of energy are one-way but experienced as dual (according to our orientation), the energies of the planets have contrary psychological qualities.

Levels of description: we now have 2/Bayt/Container forming Shabbatai/Saturn with the contrary qualities of alive and dead at the fifth sepherot of 5/Hay/Life and 3/Ghimmel/Movement forming Tsedeq/Jupiter with the contrary qualities of uncertainty and peace at the sixth sepherot of 6/Vav/Union -- defining the existential axis as a polarity or binomial. Etc.

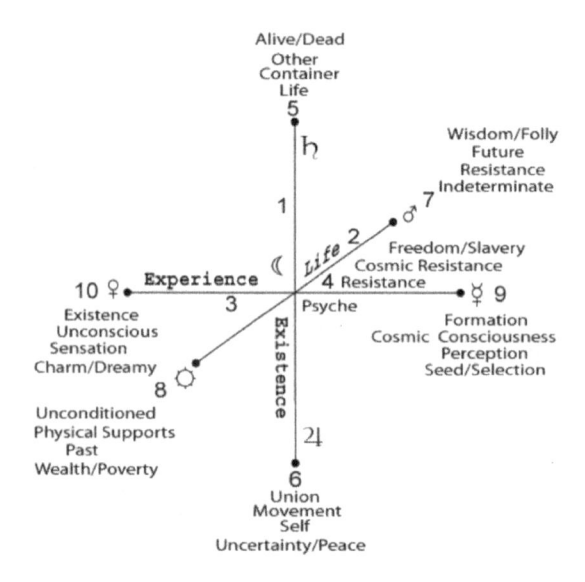

```
                    Alive/Dead
                      Other
                    Container
                      Life
                        5
                        •
                        ♄                 Wisdom/Folly
                                            Future
                    1                      Resistance
                                         Indeterminate
                                     •7
                                     ♂
                              Life 2
                         ((        Cosmic Resistance    Freedom/Slavery
   10 ♀•  Experience       4 Resistance     •☿ 9
       Existence    3    Psyche              Formation
      Unconscious       ᴱ                 Cosmic Consciousness
       Sensation       x                    Perception
      Charm/Dreamy     i                   Seed/Selection
             8 ☽       s
                       t
     Unconditioned     e
    Physical Supports  n
         Past          c    ♃
     Wealth/Poverty    e    
                        6
                       Union
                     Movement
                        Self
                  Uncertainty/Peace
```

The contrary qualities are logical alternatives for their specific spheres of emotional consciousness. Our bodies (spiritual lives) are alive or dead; our selves are uncertain or at peace. Our futures are shaped by foolish and wise choices; our past by our greedy or generous actions. Our desires are impure or pure; our responses are selective or go to seed. And the center of human psychological reality, the psyche, has no qualities at all except for the binding and release of energy.

No one seems to have noticed that the classical Virtues and Vices have a psycho-spatial organization --impatient with others, pride in self, envy shapes the future, greed the past, impure left, grasping right, depressed core -- and that the outer Sins form pairs which define axes: Anger-Pride (other-self), Envy-Greed (temporality), and Lust-Avarice (experience as feeling-thought) which determine directionality: from above to below, from front to back, and from left to right.

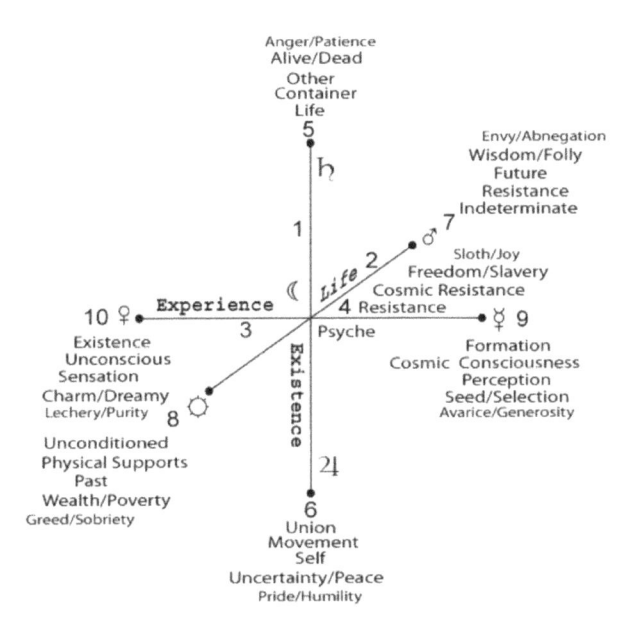

```
                    Anger/Patience
                    Alive/Dead
                        Other
                      Container
                        Life
                         5
                         •
                         ♄
                                        Envy/Abnegation
                                        Wisdom/Folly
                                            Future
                                          Resistance
                  1                      Indeterminate
                                    ♂ 7
                                  2      Sloth/Joy
                              Life     Freedom/Slavery
                          ☾          Cosmic Resistance
  10 ♀•   Experience       4 Resistance    ☿ 9
                    3      Psyche              •
   Existence                                Formation
   Unconscious          ᴱ            Cosmic Consciousness
    Sensation           ˣ                 Perception
  Charm/Dreamy   ☉      ⁱ                Seed/Selection
   Lechery/Purity  8    ˢ              Avarice/Generosity
                        ᵗ
  Unconditioned         ᵉ
Physical Supports       ⁿ     ♃
     Past               ᶜ
 Wealth/Poverty         ᵉ     6
 Greed/Sobriety               •
                            Union
                          Movement
                             Self
                       Uncertainty/Peace
                         Pride/Humility
```

With the emotional coloration of the virtues and vices, we now have five levels of interrelated meaning for each of seven psychological directions deriving from three axes and the center of the Cube. Each direction is internally consistent and logically paired with its opposite across each level.

What was called a sin in classical times we now call emotion and treat with drugs and mass entertainment. The Cube defines seven primary states of "emotional consciousness" and organizes them in psycho-spatial directions. Dante, following classical wisdom and a pre-perspective view, organized them in triads and put Sloth in the center.

Dante's Punishments:

Cold Sins: (perverted love)

1. Pride: Carrying heavy stones.

2. Envy: Sealed eyes.

3. Anger: Smoke.

Sins of Improper Measure: (defective love)

4. Sloth: Running

Warm Sins: (excessive love)

5. Avarice: Prostration.

6. Gluttony: Starvation.

7. Lust: Fire.

Stewart A. Swerdlow • 35

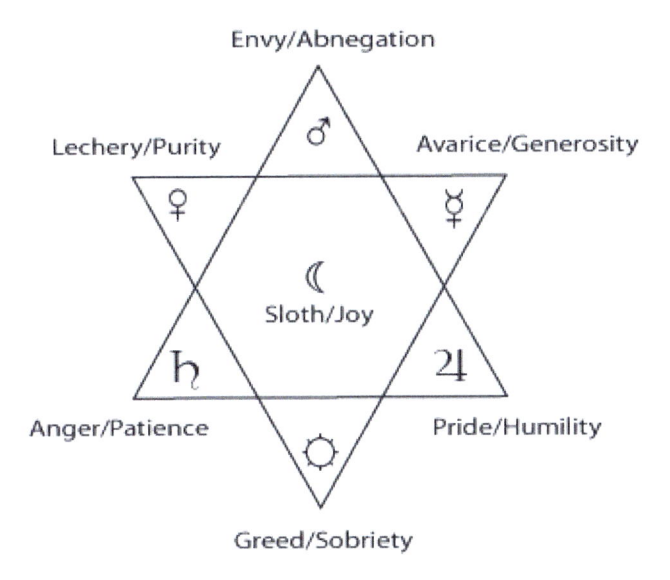

```
                    Envy/Abnegation
                         ♂
   Lechery/Purity              Avarice/Generosity
         ♀                          ☿
                   ☾
                Sloth/Joy
         ♄                          ♃
   Anger/Patience              Pride/Humility
                         ☉
                   Greed/Sobriety
```

Rotating one of the triangles of the hexagram off the page into the 3rd dimension restores their relationship in the Cube. The primary triad of 5-6-7 (body, self, future) determines the course of psychological evolution of the individual. The secondary triad of 8-9-10 (past, thought, feeling) records the experience.

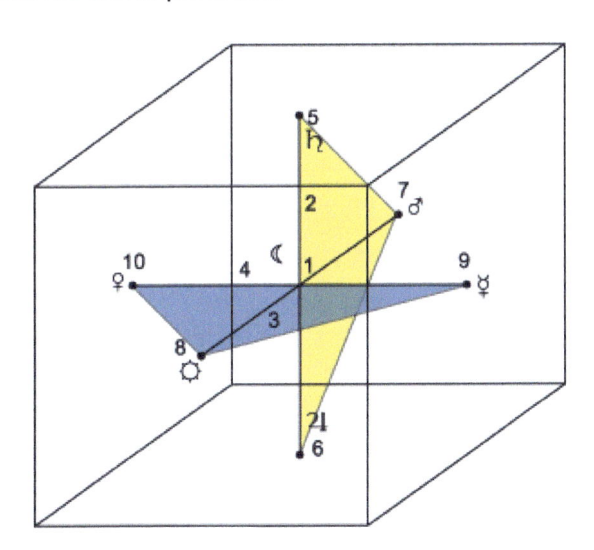

The definition of terms presents problems in thinking about the structure of consciousness or the mind-body problem. What is consciousness, awareness, perception, cognition, thought? Or sensation, feeling, desire, emotion? How are they related to each other and to the larger categories of existence, life and subjective experience?

The terms we have been using to describe the categories of the Cube of Space are translations of the precise, semantically-accurate (non-arbitrary) equations of the Sepher Yetsira. Even in translation, their consistency and logical organization is easy to see. The Cube, for all its complexity, is a "common-sense" model: its categories and structures link the psychological and experiential worlds with a psycho-spatial metaphor of emotional consciousness and psychological development that puts the individual at the center of his or her experience and organizes it in a consistent, common-sense way.

The Cube distinguishes between thought and consciousness and between feeling and emotion. The seven states of consciousness represented by the faces and center of the Cube are all emotionally qualified. Feeling itself is only one of the directions; it just happens to be the one in touch with the sensuous reality of physical existence. Both poles of experience -- sensuous reality and feeling -- and -- perception and conscious thought -- are only two of seven possible dimensions of emotional consciousness. Rather than Consciousness being the feeling of what happens, what happens and its felt experience is one of the facets of consciousness.

The Cube explodes the Cartesian dilemma with higher-dimensional geometry (a map of mind becoming matter and matter becoming mind) and by showing how mind connects with the matter of felt experience in order to actualize developmental states of consciousness.

To review, we've outlined the structure of the Cube of Space as composed of an inner space defined by the axes and center, and an outer space defined by six opposing faces. The first is timeless, the second responsible for psychological evolution and development. The seven centers of emotional consciousness (faces plus center) define the primary emotional contexts for human experience as an individual existence in development.

To complete our metapsychological outline we need to define the twelve outer edges of the Cube. What do they represent? Unlike the axes and faces, their energies do not pass through us and would evade our perception were it not for the foci of the faces. Metaphors for the boundaries of our experience, the edges describe developmental stages in the evolution and involution of energy. Defined by the intersection of the faces, the edges form active environments for the energies of the seven directions, facilitating the development of emotional consciousness in different areas of experience.

The edges describe twelve states or stages in the organization of physical and psychological energies. They define the parameters of psychological development, sometimes leading to the building up of structures, sometimes to their tearing down, depending on the direction of evolution or involution.

12 Simple Autiot (Signs): Energetic Structure of the Zodiac: Active Developmental Environments												
Toleh	Shaur	Teomaim	Sartan	Arieh	Betolah	Mozenaim	'Aqarav	Qoshet	Ghedi	Deli	Daghim
ה	ו	ז	ח	ט	י	ל	נ	ס	ע	צ	ק
5	6	7	8	9	10	30	50	60	70	90	100
♈	♉	♊	♋	♌	♍	♎	♏	♐	♑	♒	♓

Zodiac means path. The edges are pathways for the transformation of energy/consciousness, and have been interpreted in many ways, usually in circular mappings.

The circular zodiac, like the Tree of Life, is a 2-dimensional projection of the same higher dimensional object that the Cube represents in 3 dimensions. Both projections lose degrees of freedom as their semantic structure is reduced to 2 dimensions, and we miss the information contained in the third axis, which was not available to the pre-Renaissance mind, as we have seen with Dante's otherwise faithful representation of the Emotional States and their Cures. We will translate various twelve-fold cycles into 3-space and map them to the edges of the Cube for comparison.

Zodiac

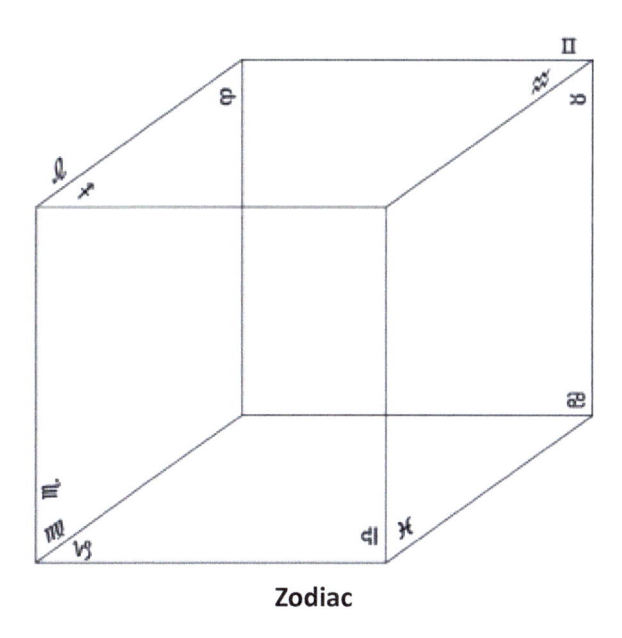

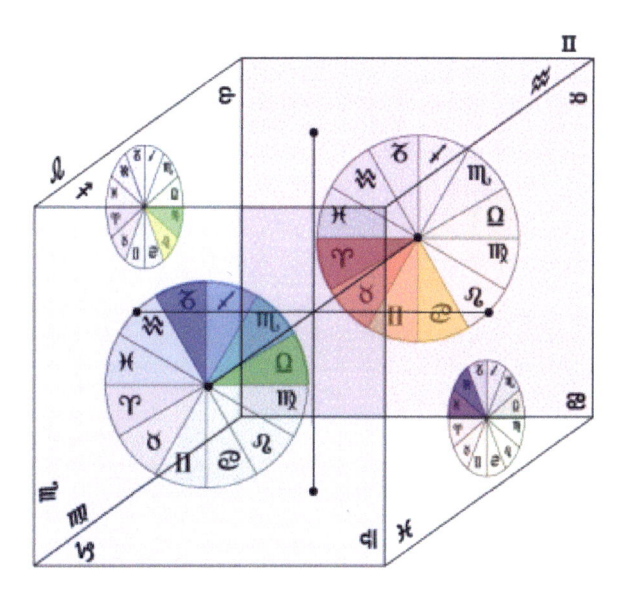

Developmental Zodiac

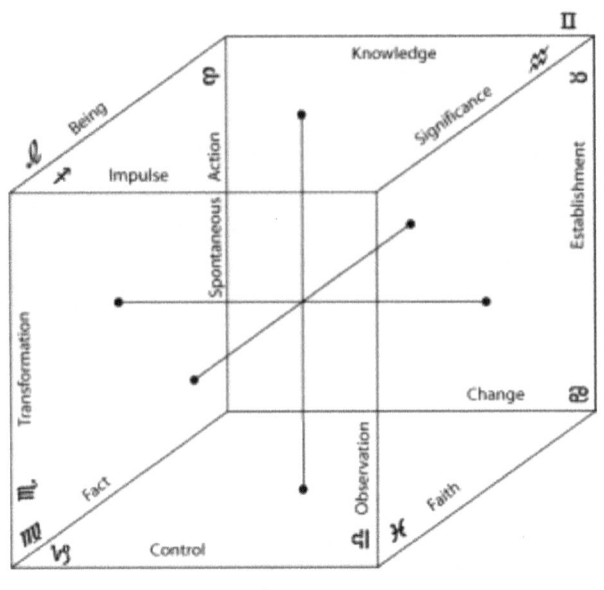

Arthur Young

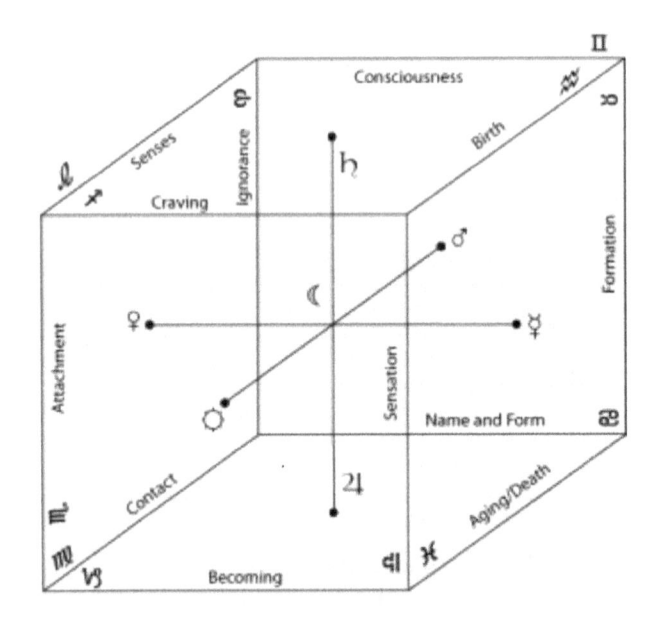

Twelve-fold Independent Co-origination

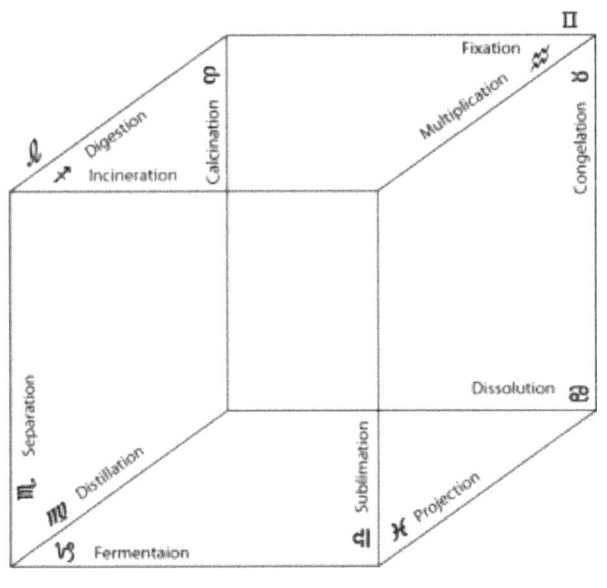

Alchemy

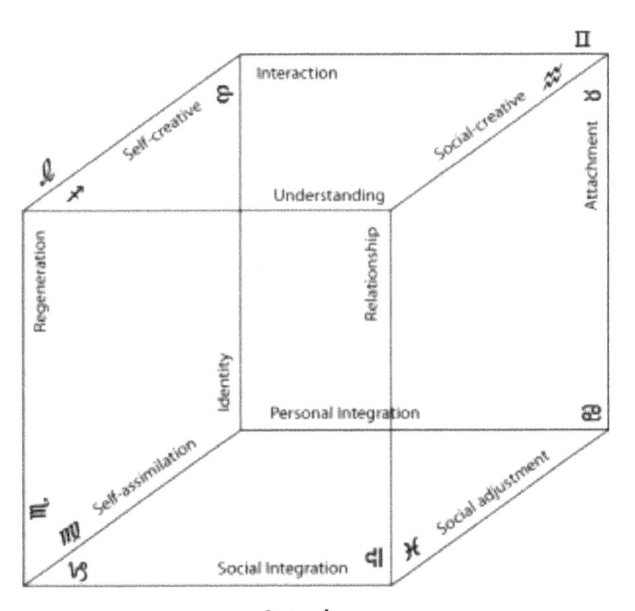

Astrology

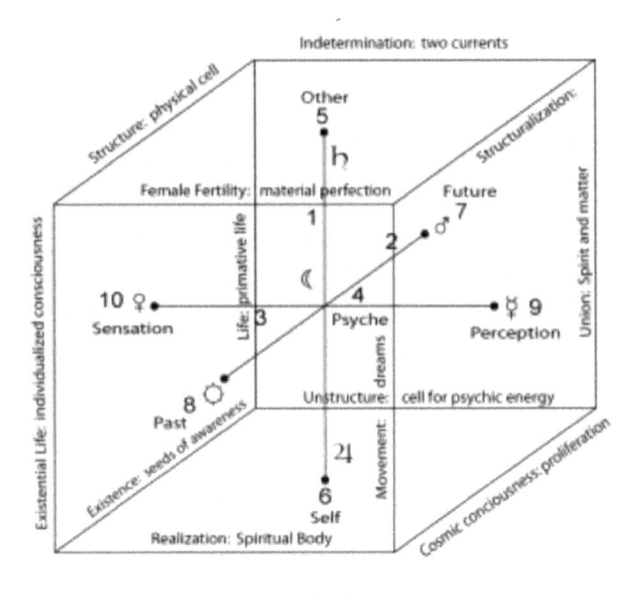

Qabala

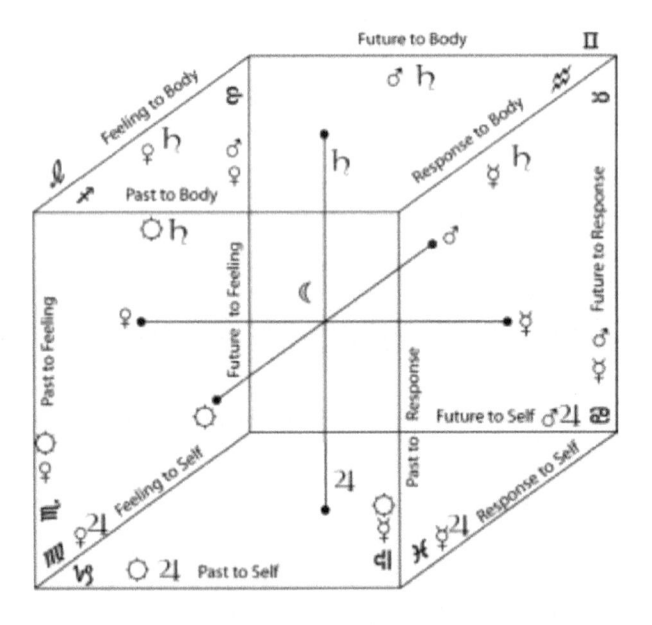

Planetary Flows

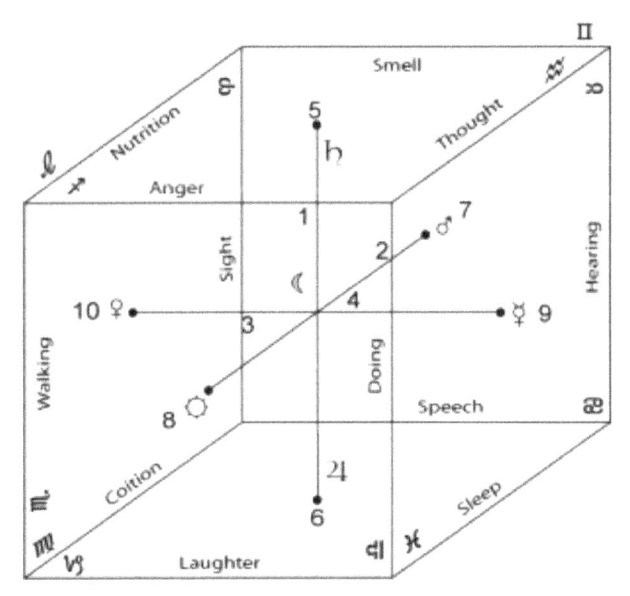

Edges of the Soul

Notes

George Lakoff: Metaphors We Live By | Metaphors We Live By

Dan J. Bruiger: The Rise and Fall of Reality: Deliberations on the Mind-Body Problem

Humberto R. Maturana: Ontology of Observing: The Biological Foundations of Self Consciousness and the Physical Domain of Existence

George Lakoff: The Theory of Cognitive Models

Daniel C. Richardson, Michael J. Spivey, Shimon Edelman, Adam J. Naples: "Language is Spatial": Experimental Evidence for Image Schemas of Concrete and Abstract Verbs

David S. Miall: The Body in Literature: Mark Johnson, Metaphor, and Feeling

Aldo Mosca: A Review Essay on Antonio Damasio's The Feeling of What Happens: Body and Emotion in the Making of Consciousness

David J. Chalmers: Facing Up to the Problem of Consciousness

David Chalmers: The Hard Problem

J Andrew Ross: The Self: From Soul to Brain

Daniel C. Dennett: Facing Backwards on the Problem of Consciousness: Commentary on Chalmers

David Brooks: How to Solve the Hard Problem: A Predictable Inexplicability

Piero Scaruffi: Thymos: Studies on Consciousness, Cognition and Life

Richard Boothby Freud as Philosopher: Metapsychology after Lacan - Reviewed by Elliot L. Jurist, CUNY - Philosophical Reviews

Natalie Angier, NYTimes: Abstract Thoughts? The Body Takes Them Literally

The best way to understand the role of Freud's metapsychology is as a two-fold set of basic, "transcendental" concepts: on the one hand, these concepts represent some of the underlying conditions of possibility for the formation and existence of human reality as it's experienced by the psyche; on the other hand, these concepts serve as possibility conditions for the analytic interpretation of this same field of human experiential reality (in short, as possibility conditions shaping both the subject of psychoanalytic investigation as well as the procedures of the agent-analyst carrying out this investigation).

Adrian Johnston: *Review of Boothby's Freud as Philosopher.*

Metapsychological: taken together, those aspects of Freud's theorizing that are economical (the hydraulics of unpleasure-avoidance through pleasure), dynamic (libido movements among id, ego, and superego), and topographic (psyche as structured into conscious, preconscious, and unconscious layers). Metapsychology also takes clinical observations beyond the consulting room and applies them to everyone, with varying results. Although psychoanalysis began as a treatment method, Freud's real interest was caught by those theorizings that applied it to human psychology in general. Referring to two recent books, Freud wrote this to his friend Oskar Pfister:

"I do not know whether you have guessed the hidden link between my "Lay Analysis" and "Illusion." In the former I want to protect analysis from physicians, and in the latter from priests. I want to entrust it to a profession that doesn't yet exist, a profession of secular ministers of souls, who don't have to be physicians and must not be priests."
Freudian Glossary

Over 100,000 Google links for "psychological space."

Mappings in the Cube of Space

Each axis is initialized by one of the three roots of the Name YHWH. The expansion of the Name in triads (3-space) creates psychological-developmental space in man. The "Sealing" of the outer directions completes the transition from inner to outer psychological space: all possible permutations of the letters Yod (existence), Hay (life) and Vav (union) taken three at a time seal the faces of the Cube. Aleph externalizes as Yod (up-down: existence), Mem as Hay (front-back: archetypal life) and Sheen as Vav (left-right: union/copulation).

The oppositions contained within each seal's triad (Yod-Hay-Waw, Yod-Waw-Hay) become explicit in the outer directions and the faces of the Cube. Each pair of opposing faces belongs to one of the three primary categories: existence, life and union. In experiential-developmental space, these categories become the polarities of self-body, future-past and sense-perception or feeling-thought and are symbolized or specified by the equations for the astrological planets and their formative letters.

Levels of Semantic Integration in the Cube

Sephirot

Stewart A. Swerdlow • 47

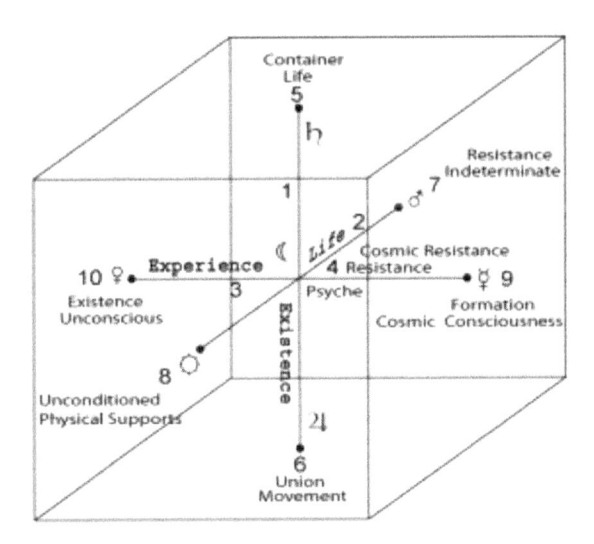

```
              Container
                Life
                 5
                 ♄
                 1
              ☾   2
          Experience  Cosmic Resistance
      10 ♀ ·   3    4 Resistance    ·☿ 9
        Existence     Psyche      Formation
        Unconscious              Cosmic Consciousness
                  8 ☉
      Unconditioned
      Physical Supports
                  ♃
                  6
                Union
              Movement
```

Resistance
Indeterminate
♂ 7

Formatives

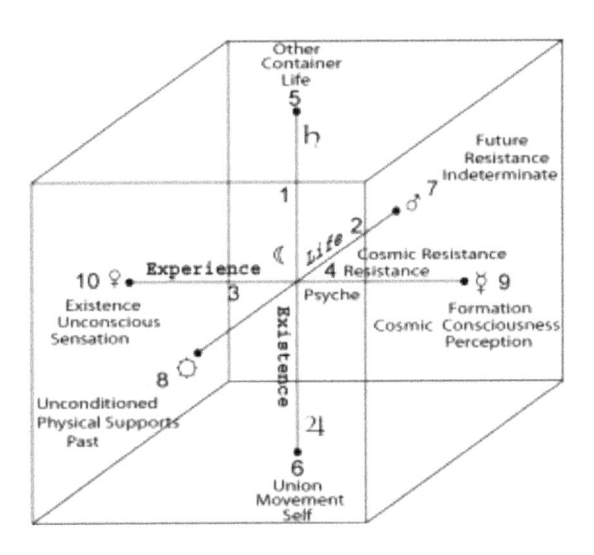

```
                Other
              Container
                Life
                 5
                 ♄
                                 Future
                                 Resistance
                 1              Indeterminate
              ☾   2              ♂ 7
          Experience  Cosmic Resistance
      10 ♀ ·   3    4 Resistance    ·☿ 9
        Existence     Psyche      Formation
        Unconscious              Cosmic Consciousness
        Sensation                 Perception
                  8 ☉
      Unconditioned
      Physical Supports
      Past
                  ♃
                  6
                Union
              Movement
                Self
```

Planets

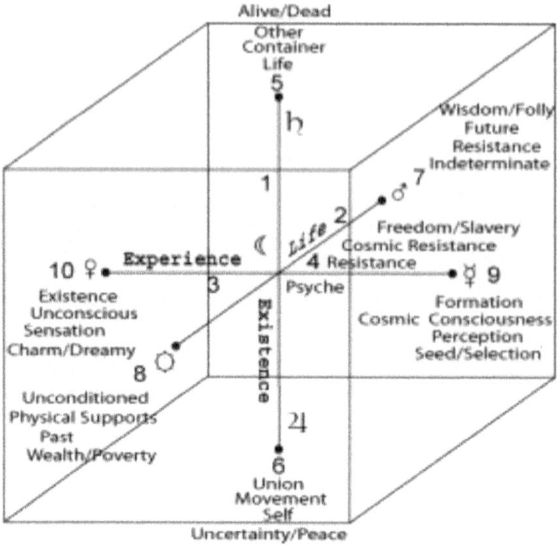
Alive/Dead
Other
Container
Life
5
Wisdom/Folly
Future
Resistance
Indeterminate
7
1
Life
2
Freedom/Slavery
Cosmic Resistance
4 Resistance
10
Experience
9
3
Psyche
Existence
Unconscious
Sensation
Charm/Dreamy
Existence
Formation
Cosmic Consciousness
Perception
Seed/Selection
8
Unconditioned
Physical Supports
Past
Wealth/Poverty
6
Union
Movement
Self
Uncertainty/Peace

Contrary Qualities

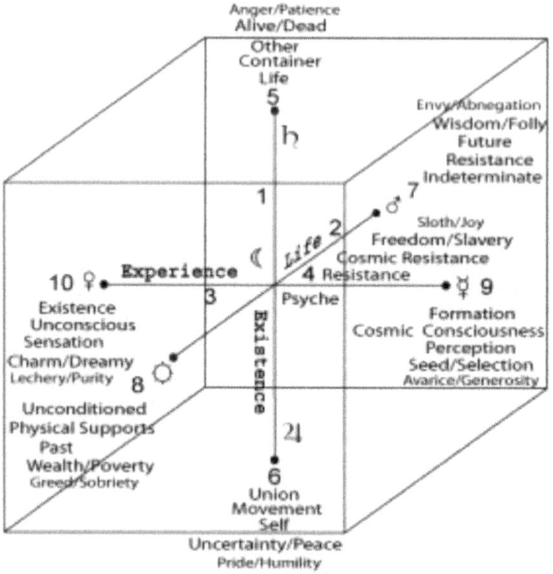
Anger/Patience
Alive/Dead
Other
Container
Life
5
Envy/Abnegation
Wisdom/Folly
Future
Resistance
Indeterminate
7
1
Sloth/Joy
Life
2
Freedom/Slavery
Cosmic Resistance
4 Resistance
10
Experience
9
3
Psyche
Existence
Unconscious
Sensation
Charm/Dreamy
Lechery/Purity
Existence
Formation
Cosmic Consciousness
Perception
Seed/Selection
Avarice/Generosity
8
Unconditioned
Physical Supports
Past
Wealth/Poverty
Greed/Sobriety
6
Union
Movement
Self
Uncertainty/Peace
Pride/Humility

Virtues & Vices

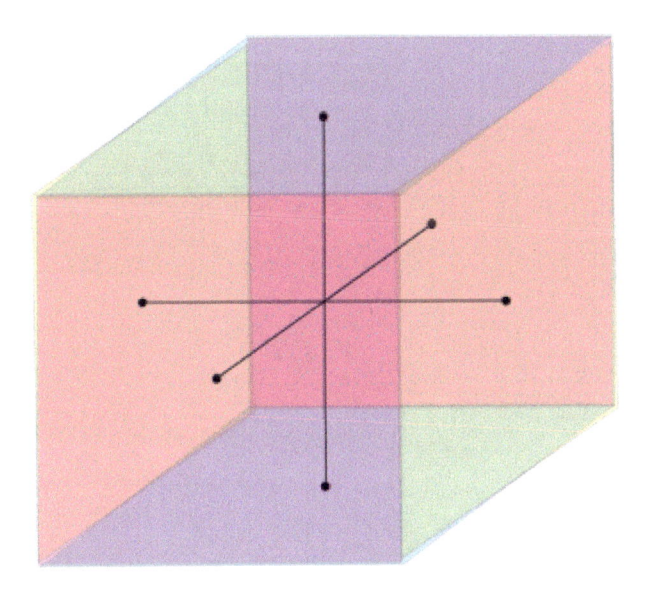

Cube Faces

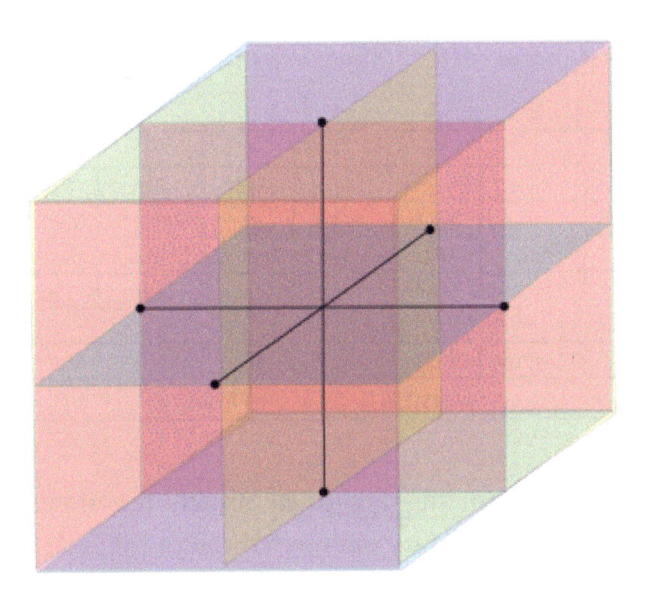

Faces + Planes

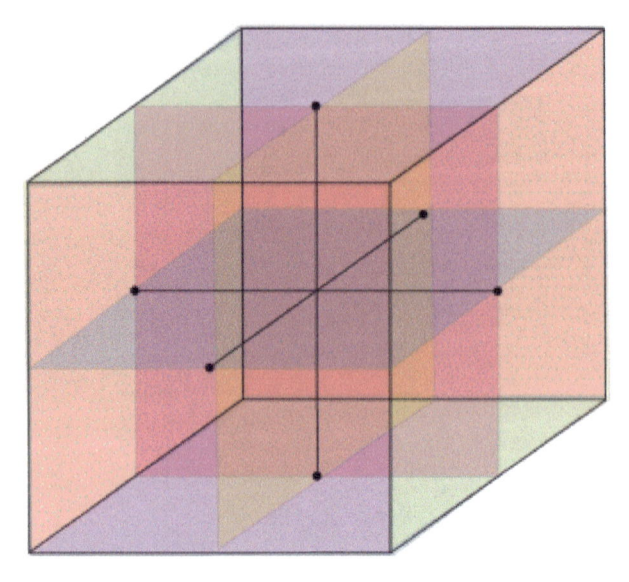

Planes + Faces + Edges

Formative Hebrew Letter /Planetary Attributions in the Cube of Space

Sephirot	5	6	7	8	9	10	
Version/etter	Bayt	Ghimmel	Dallet	Kaf	Pay	Raysh	Tav
Short Version	Saturn	Jupiter	Mars	Sun	Venus	Mercury	Moon
Gra	Moon	Mars	Sun	Venus	Mercury	Saturn	Jupiter
Golden Dawn	Mercury	Moon	Venus	Jupiter	Mars	Sun	Saturn
Ptolomy	Saturn	Jupiter	Mars	Sun	Venus	Mercury	Moon
Classical Order of the Planets							

In addition to the categories already mentioned, the linking of the planetary energies through the axes of the cube creates three sets of planetary binomial equations (Shabatai-Tsedeq: 300.2.400.10-90.4.100, etc). These are seen as two poles of one energy: Shatabai/Saturn and Tsedeq/Jupiter must be considered both in their own structures and in their relationship to each other. Their meaning is incomplete without the complement. This means that we also have to ask: -- why a particular planet with a particular planet? And that planetary "assignments" to the sephirot should be justified in terms of their oppositions in the Cube of Space. We have seen that the axes of the cube are sealed with successive permutations of Yod, Hay and Waw, representing existence, life and their union or interpenetration. In terms of an overview of the planetary energies, the Yod/existential axis connects Shabatai/Saturn/body and Tsedeq/Jupiter/self, the Hay/Life axis connects Meadim/Mars/future with Hamah/Sun/past and the Waw/Union axis connects Nogah/Venus/sensous experience with Kawkab/Mercury/sense perception. Lavanah/Moon/psyche is at the intersection of these axes. Before we ask why Saturn with Jupiter and not Moon with Mars or Mercury with Moon, we can focus on the Seal, Sephirot and Formative of the first two outer directions to put the question in the context of the linked categories of the Cube. We have already seen that the vertical, apex/deep axis defined by the 5th and 6th sephirot is sealed by the Yod of existence. This means that the two sephirot are two poles of one energy, in this case the "energy" (or "structure") of existence itself. The three polar energies are formed from the same components of existence, life and union/copulation in different combinations; the same energies considered from different perspectives. First, the 5th/Life Sephirot and the 6th/Union Sephirot, sealed with the Yod of existence, are formed by 2/Bayt/body and 3/Ghimmel/energy to establish the container/contained self-other identity of being. 2, a body, is a container for 5, life. 3, organic movement/energy of every Bayt animated by Aleph, produces the second, inner Hay, which is doubled in 6, union. At 5, the Hay of Yod emits a Waw. At 6, the Waw of Yod emits a Hay. We can see in these analogies the abstract semantic primitives, or basic formative structures, of being. The first set constitutes the vertical axis of existence, which has two poles: the existence (body) of the container and the life (energy) of the contained, which constitute identity. The second set is the front/back axis of life, which is determined by an indeterminate future and a realized past. The third is the left/right axis of union, characterized by unstructured/unconscious sensual input and (relatively) conscious/structured cognitive/perceptual response. Their intersection is the experience of living identity, or embodied being. With this context we can consider: why Saturn and Jupiter as the first binomial?

First Planetary Binomial							
5th Sephira				6th Sephira			
Height				Abyss			
2	ב	Formative		3	ג	Formative	
יהו		Seal		יוה		Seal	
Shabatai/Saturn				Tsedeq/Jupiter			
י	ת	ב	ש	צ	ד	ק	
10	400	2	300	100	4	90	
Gematria: 712				Gematria: 194			
Total: 906							
Hhaim-Mot				Shalom-Raa			
מ	ו	ת		ח	י	י	ם	ר	ע		ש	ל	ו	ם
400	6	40		40	10	10	8	70	200		40	6	30	300
446		68		270		376	
Gematria: 514				Gematria: 646			
Total: 1160							

Which is the same question as: why are Saturn and Jupiter the basic formative structures of embodied identity?

3	ג	Formative	2	ב	Formative
Tsedeq/Jupiter			Shabatai/Saturn		
ק	ר	צ	י	ת	ב	ש
100	4	90	10	400	2	300

In classical Hebrew and Ptolomaic cosmology, the second and third letter of the Hebrew alphabet bring Saturn and Jupiter, the two outermost planets and celestial spheres into being. The first letter, Aleph, which has been working its way down from Aleph-Yod-Noun, is represented here by the Sheen (300) of Shabatai in its impact on the Bayt (2) of our bodies with the goal of making them tabernacles (400) of Aleph in existence (10). This state, representing "the complete release of our vitality" in a new birth and cosmically realized freedom, is far in mankind's developmental future. And so is the union of male (100) and female (90) energies capable of producing the necessary resistance (4) to release Cosmic Aleph, the Qof of Tsedeq. In unrealized man, these energies appear as our higher aspirations and material foundations. We often find a formative or close relative imbedded in the planetary (or other) equations. Bayt is at the core of Shabatai. We find Dallet in the center of Tsedeq because it is the resistance of the structures of Tsadde that allows Qof/Cosmic Aleph to form. This resistance will be mated with Aleph and projected into an uncertain future with Meadim (Mem-Aleph-Dallet-Yod-Mem)/Mars at the 7th Sephira. It should be clear that we are dealing with basic concepts of identity and existence, both in terms of a present state and a developmental potential. Saturn and Jupiter are polar, complementary energies or structures, concerned with establishing both the foundations of existence and its purpose. The beginning and end of this process are Sheen and Qof: Aleph as Sheen/Cosmic Breath permeates our bodies and the energy of Aleph/Qof evolves through the resistant structures of Tsadde (spelled Tsadde-Dallet-Yod)-Dallet. The purpose of identity is the cosmic resurrection of Aleph as Qof. The contrary qualities of the respective planets make this even more clear. 2/Bayt forms a body for 5/Life with the energy of Shabatai. Shabatai has the contrary qualities of life and death. The contrary qualities of Tsedeq, formed by the organic movement/energy of Ghimmel/3 and the 6/Union Sephira are peace and uncertainty. A 2/body can be alive or dead. 3/Energy is at rest or unpredictable. The Sephira fits with the formative semantics of the contrary quality of the planet. The Saturn-Jupiter/vertical/existence axis is the only one that runs through the whole body from head to foot. These categories are experienced internally as other/body and self/female-male (Tsedeq: Tsadde/90-Dallet/4-Qof/100 bisexual identity.

Note the circular diagrams in the preceding information that delineate the types of consciousness within the variations of the cube form. This is literally a situation where the circle shape fits into the cube shape!

This cube form compartmentalizes as the matrix of the Oversoul, which incorporates the various lifestreams, and the realities through which they pass. These, then, create the lifetimes of each lifestream/Soul-Personality, and are the basis of each of your Simultaneous Existences.

GOD – MIND

OVERSOUL
∞

Vertical lines represent life streams

Dots represent Soul-Personalities

Horizontal lines are realities through which the life stream passes and intersects to create a lifetime.

Unfortunately, the evil entities that control the Earth use this form to create programming and mind-control.

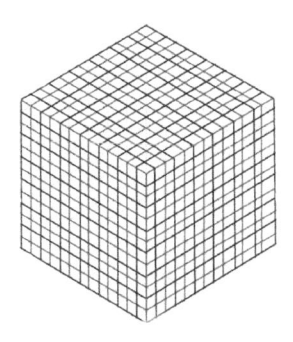

13 x 13 x 13 Programming Matrix Cube

Read *13-Cubed, 13-Cubed Squared, True Reality of Sexuality, Hyperspace Helper, Hyperspace Plus* and *Healing Archetypes and Symbols* for more information.

Spiritually, this cube is manifested as the Tfillim used by male Orthodox Jews for their morning prayers, and by Muslims who worship at the Kaaba in Mecca.

Tfillim

Kaaba

When a cube is turned so that a point is facing up, it becomes a diamond shape, which is the symbol of the Crown Chakra.

One side of a cube is a square, which is the Hyperspace symbol for Physical reality. It is also the Hebrew letter, Mem, which in Kaballah, is a vortex or opening to other dimensions.

Two forms of Mem

Mem – Sofit
Ends a word

Use in beginning
or middle of word

Section 2
History

Simbatyon

When I was a small boy, my maternal Austrian grandmother would tell me about the legend of Simbatyon. According to her, it was a mystical place in the East where a paradise existed beyond a river, and Jewish people could be free. Her father, who was a red-haired, blue-eyed Rabbi connected to the Gaon of Vilna descendants, had told her about it before he died at the age of 37.

For many years I searched for this place. I could not find it on any map. No one, in any country, had ever heard of it. I relegated the idea to some folk fantasy and let it go.

One day recently the idea came to me to look up the Hebrew meaning of Simbatyon. There was none. Then I decided to break the word apart into:

sim bat tsion

Translates into

Give the daughter of Tzion

This made me wonder if this could be a reference to the Lost Tribes who went to the East?

Then I met Maria, from my homeland of Sverdlovsk in Siberia. She also knew this legend and the following is her analysis.

Knowing about the three-letter Hebrew root words, you will see the connection too as they have many matching letters:

Sambation

Shamb(h)ala → Shanrgi-la → Zhangzhung (kingdom & culture in Tibet) → Tzimtzum → Samsung → Samson

Sarmatians – ancient Iranian tribes that left traces all over Asia.

Samaritan – one of the Hebrew tribes.

Songhua – river in China, which is the continuation of Amur River in Russia.

Amur – river in Siberia, geographically not so far from the Jewish autonomous country and places of UFO sightings in Siberia in the 20th century (and earlier).

I ended up scrolling through many wikipedia articles and found this one: https://en.wikipedia.org/wiki/Tungusic_peoples about Tungusic peoples who also have Y chromosome.

https://en.wikipedia.org/wiki/Haplogroup_Y_(mtDNA)

Haplogroup Y has been found with high frequency in many indigenous populations who live around the Sea of Okhotsk, including approximately 66% of Nivkhs, approximately 43% of Ulchs, approximately 40% of Nanais, approximately 21% of Negidals, and approximately 20% of Ainus. It is also fairly common among indigenous peoples of the Kamchatka Peninsula (Koryaks, Itelmens) and Maritime Southeast Asia.

The distribution of haplogroup Y in populations of the Malay Archipelago contrasts starkly with the absence or extreme rarity of this clade in populations of continental Southeast Asia in a manner reminiscent of haplogroup E. However, the frequency of haplogroup Y fades more smoothly away from its maximum around the Sea of Okhotsk in Northeast Asia, being found in approximately 2% of Koreans and in South Siberian and Central Asian populations with an average frequency of 1%.

> The Y2 subclade has been observed in 40% (176/440) of a large pool of samples from Nias in western Indonesia, ranging from a low of 25% (3/12) among the Zalukhu subpopulation to a high of 52% (11/21) among the Ho subpopulation.

I see many references to the Lost Tribes, Templars, maritime exploration, trade routes, piracy, etc. Although not all of it is stated directly, we can connect the dots to what we learned from Expansions.

Waugh reminds me of my mother-in-law's last name Wouw (from Dutch, German, Southern French, and possibly other Mediterranean, e.g., Portuguese ancestry) and the Hebrew letter Vov.

Hebrides also refer to the Hebrews, as you learned in the January class.

The image of the bead reminded me of the toroid shape of our planet, the universe, and the word Torah itself.

The Y group pool is extremely diverse and has proven to withstand anything. A wonder of creation!

The researcher has provided a lot of background information that I like very much.

I was lately reading about the connection between Russia/Rossiya and the Hebrew letter Rosh, which is another interesting Hebrew link.

We are indeed more than we think!

> 1) "According to the Bible, the Children of Israel conquered the Golan from the Amorites. The Bible says that the area, known as Bashan, was inhabited by two Israelite tribes during the time of Joshua, the tribe of Dan and Manasseh. The city of Golan was a city of refuge. King Solomon appointed ministers in the region. After the split of the United Monarchy, the area was contested between the northern Kingdom of Israel and the Aramean kingdom from

the 9th century BC. King Ahab of Israel (reigned 874–852 BC) defeated Ben-Hadad I in Afek of the southern Golan."

2) "Between 1891 and 1894, Baron Edmond James de Rothschild purchased around 150,000 dunams of land in the Golan and the Hawran for Jewish settlement. Legal and political permits were secured and ownership of the land was registered in late 1894.

3) A picture of Nimrod fortress

Looks like that's another extra-dimensional border that needs protection (a 'wall' or shield of some sort).

Incorporating Maria's analysis into my translation of Simbatyon it seems that Simbatyon has to do with the "Daughters of Zion" who fled during the Assyrian invasion of 732 BC, or during the Babylonian invasion of 587 BC. When the Persians invaded Babylon and freed the Hebrews, instead of going back to Israel, some went North and some East, bringing their genetics with them, as described in the analysis.

Mystery solved? Let's look at history and the flow of the Lost Tribes.

Hebrew DNA Flow

There are over 2 billion people on Earth who have Hebrew DNA and do not know it. This information is specifically designed to show the flow of the Hebrews into the global population. The following is a list of the 12 Tribes of Israel. You will see that the truth is not what you were taught.

Twelve Tribes of Israel From Wikipedia

According to the Hebrew Bible, the **Twelve Tribes of Israel** or **Tribes of Israel** (Hebrew: שבטי ישראל) descended from the 12 sons of the patriarch Jacob (who was later named Israel) and his two wives, Leah and Rachel, and two concubines, Zilpah and Bilhah.

Map of the Twelve Tribes of Israel

Deuteronomy 33:6–25 lists the twelve tribes:

Reuben

Simeon

Levi

Judah

Issachar

Zebulun

Dan

Naphtali

Gad

Asher

Joseph (including Ephraim and Manasseh)

Benjamin

Jacob elevated the descendants of Ephraim and Manasseh (the two sons of Joseph and his Egyptian wife Asenath) to the status of full tribes in their own right due to Joseph receiving a double portion after Reuben lost his birth right because of his transgression with Bilah.

In the biblical narrative, the period from the conquest of Canaan under the leadership of Joshua until the formation of the first Kingdom of Israel, passed with the tribes forming a loose confederation, described in the Book of Judges. Modern scholarship has called into question the beginning, middle, and end of this picture and the account of the conquest under Joshua has largely been abandoned. The Bible's depiction of the 'period of the Judges' is widely considered doubtful. The extent to which a united Kingdom of Israel ever existed is also a matter of ongoing dispute.

Living in exile in the sixth century BCE, the prophet Ezekiel has a vision for the restoration of Israel, of a future utopia in which the twelve tribes of Israel are living in their land again.

In the Christian New Testament, the twelve tribes of Israel are referred to twice in the gospels and twice in the Book of Revelation. In Matthew, paralleled by Luke, Jesus anticipates that in the Kingdom of God, his followers will "sit on [twelve] thrones, judging the twelve tribes of Israel". In the vision of the writer of the Book of Revelation, 144,000 of all the tribes of the children of Israel were "sealed", 12,000 from each tribe and in his vision of the New or Heavenly Jerusalem, the tribes' names were written on the city gates:

The names of the twelve tribes of the children of Israel: three gates on the east, three gates on the north, three gates on the south, and three gates on the west.[18]

Quran states that the people of Moses were split into twelve tribes. Chapter 7 verse 160 says:

"We split them up into twelve tribal communities, and We revealed to Moses, when his people asked him for water, [saying], 'Strike the rock with your staff,' whereat twelve fountains gushed forth from it. Every tribe came to know its drinking-place. And We shaded them with clouds, and We sent down to them manna and quails: 'Eat of the good things We have provided you.' And they did not wrong Us, but they used to wrong [only] themselves."

Attributed coats of arms

Attributed arms are Western European coats of arms given retrospectively to persons real or fictitious who died before the start of the age of heraldry in the latter half of the 12th century.

Attributed arms of the Twelve Tribes by Thesouro de Nobreza, 1675

Asher

Benjamin

Dan

Ephraim

Gad

Issachar

Judah

Manasseh

Naphtali	**Reuben**
Simeon	**Zebulun**

In any case, it is now widely agreed that the so-called 'patriarchal/ancestral period' is a later 'literary' construct, not a period in the actual history of the ancient world. The same is the case for the 'exodus' and the 'wilderness period,' and more and more widely for the 'period of the Judges.'" *Paula M. McNutt (1 January 1999). Reconstructing the Society of Ancient Israel. Westminster John Knox Press. p. 42. ISBN 978-0-664-22265-9.*

Alan T. Levenson (16 August 2011). The Making of the Modern Jewish Bible: How Scholars in Germany, Israel, and America Transformed an Ancient Text. Rowman & Littlefield Publishers. p. 202. ISBN 978-1-4422-0518-5.

Besides the rejection of the Albrightian 'conquest' model, the general consensus among OT scholars is that the Book of Joshua has no value in the historical reconstruction. They see the book as an ideological retrojection from a later period — either as early as the reign of Josiah or as late as the Hasmonean period." *K. Lawson Younger*

Jr. (1 October 2004). "Early Israel in Recent Biblical Scholarship." In David W. Baker; Bill T. Arnold. The Face of Old Testament Studies: A Survey of Contemporary Approaches. Baker Academic. p. 200. ISBN 978-0-8010-2871-7.

It behooves us to ask, in spite of the fact that the overwhelming consensus of modern scholarship is that Joshua is a pious fiction composed by the deuteronomistic school, how does and how has the Jewish community dealt with these foundational narratives, saturated as they are with acts of violence against others?" *Carl S. Ehrlich (1999). "Joshua, Judaism and Genocide." Jewish Studies at the Turn of the Twentieth Century, Volume 1: Biblical, Rabbinical, and Medieval Studies. BRILL. p. 117. ISBN 90-04-11554-4.*

Recent decades, for example, have seen a remarkable reevaluation of evidence concerning the conquest of the land of Canaan by Joshua. As more sites have been excavated, there has been a growing consensus that the main story of Joshua, that of a speedy and complete conquest (e.g. Josh. 11.23: 'Thus Joshua conquered the whole country, just as the LORD had promised Moses') is contradicted by the archaeological record, though there are indications of *some* destruction and conquest at the appropriate time. *Adele Berlin; Marc Zvi Brettler (17 October 2014). The Jewish Study Bible (Second ed.). Oxford University Press. p. 951. ISBN 978-0-19-939387-9.*

The biblical text does not shed light on the history of the highlands in the early Iron I. The conquest and part of the period of the judges narratives should be seen, first and foremost, as a Deuteronomist construct that used myths, tales, and etiological traditions in order to convey the theology and territorial ideology of the late monarchic author(s) (e.g., Nelson 1981; Van Seters 1990; Finkelstein and Silberman 2001, 72-79, Römer 2007, 83-90)." *Israel Finkelstein (2013). The Forgotten Kingdom: The Archaeology and History of Northern Israel (PDF). Society of Biblical Literature. p. 24. ISBN 978-1-58983-912-0.*

In short, the so-called 'period of the judges' was probably the creation of a person or persons known as the deuteronomistic historian." *J. Clinton McCann (2002). Judges. Westminster John Knox Press. p. 5. ISBN 978-0-8042-3107-7.*

Although most scholars accept the historicity of the united monarchy (although not in the scale and form described in the Bible; see Dever 1996; Na'aman 1996; Fritz 1996, and bibliography there), its existence has been questioned by other scholars (see Whitelam 1996b; see also Grabbe 1997, and bibliography there). The scenario described below suggests that some important changes did take place at the time." *Avraham Faust (1 April 2016). Israel's Ethnogenesis: Settlement, Interaction, Expansion and Resistance. Routledge. p. 172. ISBN 978-1-134-94215-2.*

In some sense most scholars today agree on a 'minimalist' point of view in this regard. It does not seem reasonable any longer to claim that the united monarchy ruled over most of Palestine and Syria." *Gunnar Lebmann (2003). Andrew G. Vaughn; Ann E. Killebrew, eds. Jerusalem in Bible and Archaeology: The First Temple Period. Society of Biblical Lit. p. 156. ISBN 978-1-58983-066-0.*

There seems to be a consensus that the power and size of the kingdom of Solomon, if it ever existed, has been hugely exaggerated." *Philip R. Davies (18 December 2014). "Why do we Know about Amos?." In Diana Vikander Edelman; Ehud Ben Zvi. The Production of Prophecy: Constructing Prophecy and Prophets in Yehud. Routledge. p. 71. ISBN 978-1-317-49031-9.*

Note in the preceding information, the Tribe of Joseph split into two others—Ephraim and Manasseh. Thus, there were actually 13 Tribes, not 12!

Also note the lands attributed to the various Tribes. These lands encompass all of the current West Bank, Golan Heights, and even across the Jordan River to what is now the Kingdom of Jordan.

The emblem for the Tribe of Dan in the Tribal Coats of Arms is exactly like the German National symbol! Dan-ube River, Dan-Zig, and Dan-mark are all named after the Lost Tribe of Dan.

The emblem of the Tribe of Judah also remarkably resembles the symbols on many European Coats of Arms! These are not simply coincidences.

In Hebrew Gematria, as explained in *The Template of God-Mind* you know that words with the same letters or values are energetically connected and related. The Hebrew word for "Tribe" is Shevet. שבט

This is connected to Shabat = שבת

"Sabbath." = live is a related word שב

The second part of "Shevet" is "vet" or sometimes written as "bet."

Bet=Daughter בת

This is also connected to Bayit=House/Home=בית

"Bet" is part of "Bayit" = House/Home

This explains the Ancient Hebrew/Spiritual concept that says:

Daughters/females create the home and life of the tribe.

Jewish society is Matriarchal.

So, it is no wonder that the matriarchal mitochondrial DNA is used to discover the descendants of the Hebrew Tribes globally.

Africa

When the Assyrian armies invaded the Northern Kingdom of Israel in 732 BC, they destroyed everything; most of the population fled elsewhere. The Assyrians were considered to be the first terrorists on Earth. The ISIS Terror Group was comprised of their descendants with the additional layer of mind-control by intelligence agencies.

At that time, there were two kingdoms. The Kingdom of Israel in the North was comprised of 10 Tribes. The Kingdom of Judah in the South, which included Jerusalem, had only two Tribes. In 587 BC, the Babylonians invaded Judah and destroyed the First Temple. Most of the Jews were taken back to Babylon in captivity for 70 years until the Persians invaded Babylon and King Cyrus freed the Jews.

During the second invasion by the Babylonians, many Hebrews also fled elsewhere, including Africa.

Nigerian Professor O. Alaezi went to great lengths to research historical information about the presence of Jews in Nigeria, of which he claims to be one. His data is based mainly on the Ibos/Igbos of West Africa.

Professor Alaezi refers to his people as, "Hebrew exiles from Israel." What follows are bullet points of his research.

- *Ibos/Igbos* are Hebrews.
- 500 feet below the town of Agulu, a bronze Star of David was found in the 1940s.
- Moses married a Cushite/Ethiopian woman and had Black children with her.
- Ibo males are circumcised on the eighth day after birth/Brit Milah.
- Ibos do not eat pork.
- The Europeans called the slaves of West Africa "Heebos."
- The following people are considered to be Jewish: Ibos of Nigeria, Tutsis of East Africa, Bamilikis of Cameroon, plus the tribes of Burundi, Benin, Ghana, South Africa, and Ethiopia.
- It is estimated that over 25% of African-Americans are of Jewish descent.
- The name *Benin* comes from the Hebrew *Benim*=Sons.
- The name *Ghana* comes from the Hebrew *Gan*=Garden.
- The name *Ibo/Igbo* comes from the Hebrew *Ibrit/Ivrit*=Hebrew.
- Over 85% of the names of Ibo villages are Hebrew words.
- The Ibos claim they are descendants of the Hebrews who fled the destruction of the First Temple in 587 BC.
- Many Igbo words are actually Hebrew.
- Many claim they come from the Tribes of Gad, Judah, and Levi.
- The surname *Eze*=Ruler.
- The Igbos created the Eri Kingdom. Eri comes from the Hebrew word *Ari*, which means Lion.

- Ancient writing on the floors of buildings in Nigeria were analyzed by Israeli scientists/researchers to be ancient Hebrew.
- It is estimated that the first Hebrews arrived in Nigeria about 3000 years ago, during the time of Solomon. Remember Solomon's flying car.
- Some West Africans claim decadency from the Tribes of Reuben and Benjamin.
- Biblically, after Sarah died, Abraham married Keturah, a Black woman, and had six sons with her. This is written in the Torah.
- The New Yam Festival in West Africa is almost identical to the Jewish holiday of Sukkot.
- The British feared the Ibos and knew they were Hebrews, so they enslaved them.
- The Old Testament says that Jacob's wives Bilah and Zilpah were Black.
- In the late 1960s, the Igbos tried to create their own nation called *Biafra*. They wanted to all emigrate to Israel.
- The name *Biafra* comes from the Hebrew words *B'Afuah*, which means *in the apple*. This is a reference to Adam and Eve.
- The Ibos, when praying, use the term *Alu Le Yah*, which comes from the Hebrew *Hallelujah*, which means *Praise be to God*.
- The Igbo and other African Jews wish to be reunited in Israel as part of the Lost Tribes. So far, only the Ethiopian Falasha Jews have done so.
- It is estimated that there are 40+ million Black Jews in Africa.
- In Nigeria, an onyx stone was dug up with an inscription from the Tribe of Gad.

In the United States, there are groups of Blacks who claim to be the original Hebrews. They are based in Chicago, Miami, Los Angeles, and New York. Many of these Black Jews have gone to Israel and asked for citizenship under the Israeli "Law of Return." Most of them have been denied as not having any proof. However, with the new information coming out of Nigeria and other African nations, this may soon change.

It is no wonder, that as we enter into Messianic/End Times, the African people are starting to find out who/what they really are. It is also no surprise that Israeli Prime Minister Netanyahu has spent years reconnecting Israel to most Black African nations diplomatically.

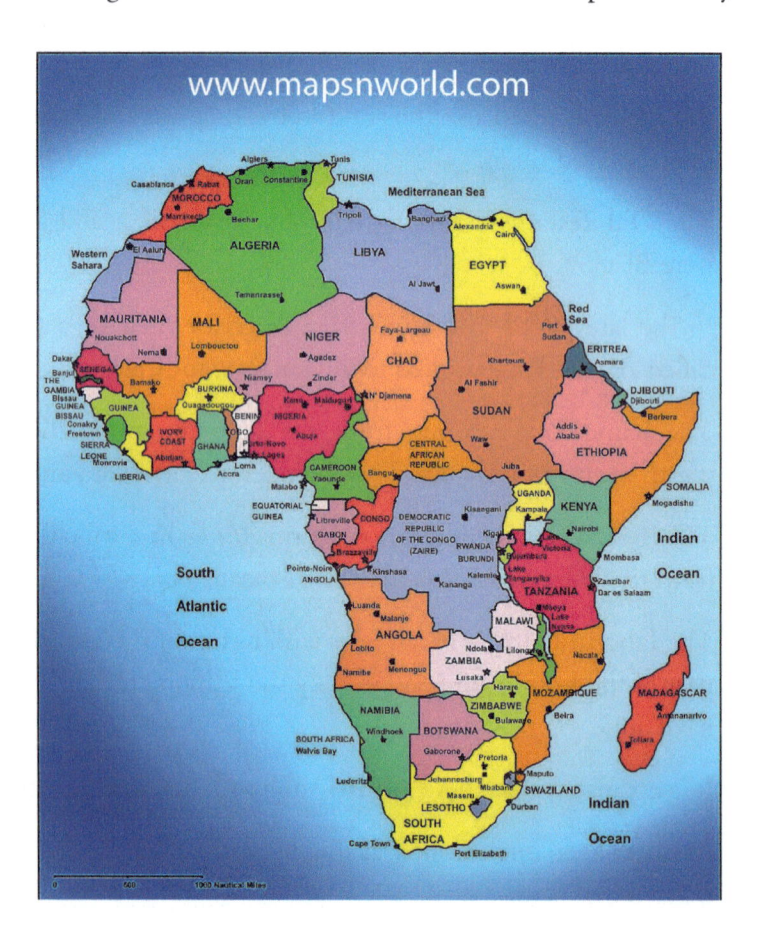

Jews of Africa

In the course of my extensive research, I often come across rare and little known works that have either never been published, or are out of print. These are treasures that often contain information that has been kept hidden, forgotten, purposefully removed from the public, or simply cast aside. The older the work, the more details it holds that are no longer available in our time.

I have found such a treasure in a salvaged book written over 100 years ago called *Jews of Africa*. It was written by a man named Sydney Mendelssohn, from England, the son of Jewish parents.

Mendelssohn found his fortune in South Africa as a diamond merchant during the late 1800s and very early 1900s. He spent decades all over Africa, learning the history of the people and especially about his own people, the Jews.

Mendelssohn returned to London to write down the information he uncovered and passed away in 1917. This particular work was posthumously published in 1920, but quickly fell into obscurity until it was found in the California library of a university and salvaged for posterity.

Much of what he wrote was a bit tedious, going over the daily activities of Jewish communities, their dress, their food and customs, and their persecutions at the hands of various rulers. However, there were some salient points that need to be remembered and added to the annals of history.

There was a huge Hebrew Kingdom in Abyssinia/Ethiopia for centuries following the return of Queen Sheba to her kingdom with her son by King Solomon, Menelik I.

A huge Hebrew kingdom existed in the mountains of Ethiopia even after the arrival of the Arabs and Europeans. Apparently, this Jewish nation was gigantic with millions of Jews who were fierce warriors and existed up to and past the Middle Ages.

The Jews that fled the Babylonian invasion of Israel in 587 BC went to North Africa, where they mixed with and converted the local tribes to Judaism in what is now Tunisia, Algeria, and Morocco. The Berbers claimed to have a Jewish Queen who was very powerful.

The Berbers were Jews until the Arab invasions in the 600s AD, but retained Jewish beliefs and traditions even after the invasion.

Yemen had a large Jewish population since the Assyrian invasion of Israel in 732 BC. Yemeni Jews connected to and enhanced the Ethiopian Jewish Kingdom.

Jewish villages and cities were found across Egypt, Libya, Tunisia, Algeria, and Morocco, even extending to Mauritania. This is why many Jews fled invasions in the Holy Land and went to Africa; their people were already there.

During the Inquisition, many Jews from Spain and Portugal fled to North Africa, where the Muslims welcomed them because the Jews already there were prosperous in commerce and banking.

Some Islamic Sultans actually hired Jews as Ambassadors to European nations because they were good intermediaries between Christianity and Islam.

Of course, there were times when the Muslims persecuted the Jews in North Africa, but always, they allowed them to stay because the Jews enhanced the country.

Ironically, some of the Muslim rulers actually sent Jewish ambassadors to the very nations that had expelled them!

The Turks under the Ottoman Empire also invaded North Africa and gave the Jews more freedoms than before. Yes, they also persecuted them at times, but generally, the Turks were fair to the Jews.

Jews from the Roman Empire, Baghdad, and France also immigrated to North Africa in large numbers for centuries.

When the French took control of North Africa in the 1800s the Jews were given equal rights and were protected from persecution. This came to an end with the close of World War II and the independence given to North African Muslim nations that then expelled Jews when Israel was re-created in 1948.

Most of history does not recognize the vast Jewish influence in Africa and their contributions to the development of kingdoms and industries on that continent. The advent of Islamic nationalism altered historical versions and erased many truths.

Today, there are literally millions of people in Africa who are either unaware of their Hebrew DNA or keep it secret for security reasons.

On the following page is a map where Hebrew refugees settled across North Africa, Europe, and Asia after various ancient invasions of Israel.

80 • Revelations of Time & Space, History and God

North Africa and the Middle East

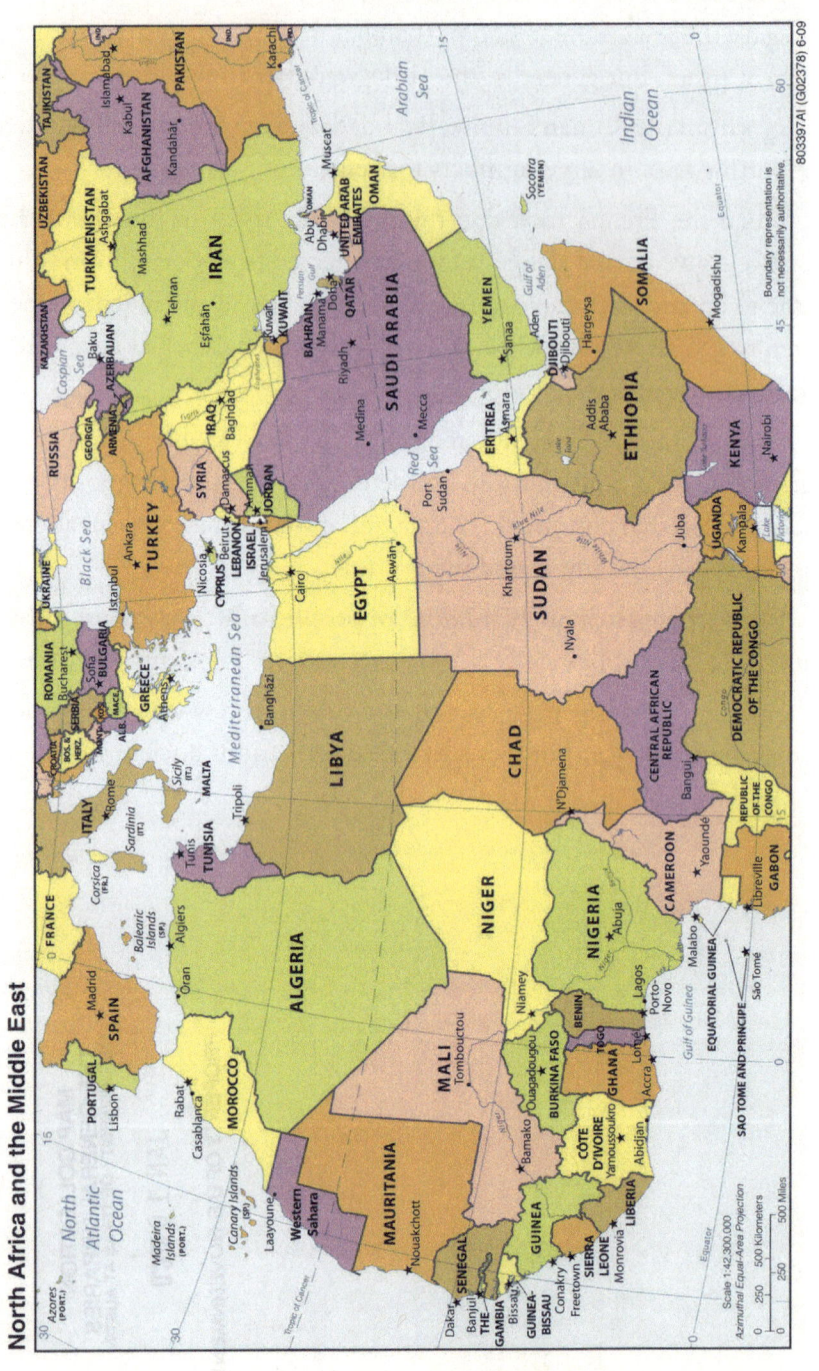

(Courtesy of Google Search and Mapsland)

Rome/Latins

To understand the flow of events, it is necessary to review the Old Testament story about Jacob and Esau, and their father, Isaac.

Jacob and Esau, From Wikipedia, the free encyclopedia

The Book of Genesis speaks of the relationship between fraternal twins Jacob and Esau, sons of Isaac and Rebekah, focusing on Esau's loss of his birthright to Jacob and the conflict that ensued between their descendant nations because of Jacob's deception of their aged and blind father, Isaac, in order to receive Esau's birthright/blessing from Isaac.

This conflict was paralleled by the affection the parents had for their favored child: "Isaac, who had a taste for wild game, loved Esau, but Rebekah loved Jacob." (Genesis 25:28). Even since conception, their conflict was foreshadowed: "And the children struggled together within her; and she said, If it be so, why am I thus? And she went to enquire of the LORD. And the LORD said unto her, Two nations are in thy womb, and two manner of people shall be separated from thy bowels; and the one people shall be stronger than the other people; and the elder shall serve the younger." (Genesis 25:22–23)

Genesis 25:26 states that Esau was born before Jacob, who came out holding on to his older brothers heel as if he was trying to pull Esau back into the womb so that he could be firstborn. The name Jacob means he grasps the heel which is a Hebrew idiom for deceptive behavior.

Birthright

In Genesis, Esau returned to his brother, Jacob, being famished from the fields. He begged his twin brother to give him some "red pottage" (paralleling his nickname, Hebrew: אדום (adom, meaning "red"). Jacob offered to give Esau a bowl of stew in exchange for his birthright (the right to be recognized as firstborn) and Esau agreed.

The birthright (bekorah) has to do with both position and inheritance. By birthright, the firstborn son inherited the leadership of the family and the judicial authority of his father. Deuteronomy 21:17 states that he was also entitled to a double portion of the paternal inheritance.

Esau acts impulsively. As he did not value his birthright over a bowl of lentil stew, by his actions, Esau demonstrates that he does not deserve to be the one who continues Abraham's responsibilities and rewards under God's covenant, since he does not have the steady, thoughtful qualities which are required.

Jacob shows his wiliness as well as his greater intelligence and forethought. What he does is not quite honorable, though not illegal. The birthright benefit that he gains is at least partially valid, although he is insecure enough about it to conspire later with his mother to deceive his father so as to gain the blessing for the first-born as well.

Later, Esau marries two wives, both Hittite women, that is, locals, in violation of Abraham's (and God's) injunction not to take wives from among the Canaanite population.

Again, one gets the sense of a headstrong person who acts impulsively, without sufficient thought (Genesis 26:34–35). His marriage is described as a vexation to both Rebekah and Isaac. Even his father, who has strong affection for him, is hurt by his act. According to Daniel J. Elazar this action alone forever rules out Esau as the bearer of patriarchal continuity. Esau could have overcome the sale of his birthright; Isaac was still prepared to give him the blessing due the firstborn. But acquiring foreign wives meant the detachment of his children from the Abrahamic line. Despite the deception on the part of Jacob and his mother to gain Isaac's patriarchal blessing, Jacob's vocation as Isaac's legitimate heir in the continued founding of the Jewish people is reaffirmed. Elazar suggests that the Bible indicates that a bright, calculating person who, at times, is less than honest, is preferable as a founder over a bluff, impulsive one who cannot make discriminating choices.

Blessing of the firstborn

Pronouncing the blessing was considered to be the act formally acknowledging the firstborn as the principal heir.

In Genesis 27:5–7, Rebecca overhears Isaac tell Esau, "Bring me venison and prepare a savory food, that I may eat, and bless thee before the LORD before my death." Rebecca councils Jacob to pretend to be Esau, in order to obtain the blessing in his brother's stead. He dressed himself in Esau's best clothes and disguised himself by covering his arms in lamb skin so that if his blind father touched him, he would think Jacob his more hirsute brother. Jacob brought Isaac a dish of goat meat prepared by Rebecca to taste like venison. Isaac then bestowed the blessing (bekhorah), which confers a prophetic wish for fertility (vv. 27–28) and dominion (v.29), on Jacob before Esau's return.

Esau is furious and vows to kill Jacob (Genesis 27:41) as soon as their father has died. Rebekah intervenes to save her younger son Jacob from being murdered by her elder son, Esau. At Rebekah's urging, Jacob flees to a distant land to work for his mother's brother, Laban (Genesis 28:5). She explains to Isaac that she has sent Jacob to find a wife among her own people.

Jacob does not immediately receive his father's inheritance. Jacob, having fled for his life, leaves behind the wealth of Isaac's flocks and land and tents in Esau's hands. Jacob is forced to sleep out on the open ground and then work for wages as a servant in Laban's household. Jacob, who had deceived his father, is in turn deceived and cheated by his relative Laban concerning Jacob's seven years of service (lacking money for a dowry) for the hand of Laban's daughter Rachel, receiving his older daughter Leah instead. However, despite Laban, Jacob eventually becomes so rich as to incite the envy of Laban and Laban's sons.

Reconciliation

Genesis 32–33 tells of Jacob and Esau's eventual meeting according to God's commandment in Genesis 31:3, 32:10 after Jacob had spent more than 20 years staying with Laban in Padan-Aram. The two men prepare for their meeting like warriors about to enter into battle. Jacob divides his family into two camps such that if one is taken the other might escape (Genesis 32:8-9). Jacob sends messengers to Esau, as well as gifts meant to appease him. Jacob gets the name Israel after he wrestles with the Angel of God as he is traveling to Esau. His hip is knocked out of joint but he keeps on wrestling and gains the name. After the encounter with the angel, Jacob crosses over the ford Jabbok and encounters Esau who seems initially pleased to see him (Genesis 33:4), which attitude of favour Jacob fosters by means of his gift. Esau refuses the gift at first but Jacob humbles himself before his brother and presses him to take it, which he finally does (Genesis 33:3, 33:10-11). However, Jacob evidently does not trust his brother's favour to continue for long so he makes excuses to avoid traveling to Mount Seir in Esau's company (Genesis 33:12-14), and he further evades Esau's attempt to put his own men among Jacob's bands (Genesis 33:15-16), and finally completes the deception of his brother yet again by going to Succoth and then to Shalem, a city of Shechem, instead of following Esau at a distance to Seir (Genesis 33:16-20). The next time Jacob and Esau meet is at the burial of their father, Isaac, in Hebron (Genesis 35:27-29). The so-called reconciliation is thus only superficial and temporary.

Views of the birthright

The narrative of Esau selling his birthright to Jacob, in Genesis 25, states that Esau despised his birthright. However, it also alludes to Jacob being thrifty.

In Esau's mother and father's eyes, the deception may have been deserved. Rebekah later abets Jacob in receiving his father's blessing disguised as Esau. Isaac then refuses to take Jacob's blessing back after learning he was tricked, and does not give this blessing to Esau but, after Esau begs, gives him an inferior blessing (Genesis 27:34–40).

References]
Attridge & Meeks. The Harper Collins Study Bible,
(ISBN 0060786841, ISBN 978-0-06-078684-7), 2006, p. 40
Genesis 25:26 footnote
Duffy, Daniel. "Esau." The Catholic Encyclopedia. Vol. 5. New York: Robert Appleton Company, 1909. 12 Jul. 2013
Easton, M.G. Illustrated Bible Dictionary, Third Ed., Thomas Nelson, 1897

Elazar, Daniel J., "Jacob and Esau and the Emergence of the Jewish People", Jerusalem Center for Public Affairs
"Firstborn", Jewish Virtual Library
"Esau", Jewish Encyclopedia
Manns OFM, Frederick. "Jacob and Esau: Rebecca's Children", American Catholic.org. Archived 2013-12-24 at the Wayback Machine
In Biblical Hebrew the name "Israel" means one who wrestles with God. See also Jacob's Ladder.

According to the Old Testament, the descendants of Esau formed a nation to the Southeast of Israel, in what is now Southern Jordan. These people were known in ancient times as the Edomites or Idumeans as well as "the secret ones."

When Babylon invaded the Southern Kingdom of Judah in 587 BC, Edom was also attacked and destroyed. According to the Kabballah and Zohar information, the remnants of Esau/Edom fled to the Mediterranean Region.

The story of the twins, Esau and Jacob, evolved into the story of the twins, Romulus and Remus, born of a wolf. Esau was born covered in thick red hair like a wolf! The Legend of Rome and the Latin people was actually derived from the ancient Hebrew stories by the Hebrew-speaking Edomites.

In ancient Hebrew, the word *Latyon* = Dwelling place of the hiding ones!

The word *Latin* means the secret ones!

The father of all Latins was a descendant of Esau named Aeneas. The name Aeneas comes from the Hebrew words/name *Ayin I jah*, which means "Eye of God."

The ancient Rabbis knew the lineage of the Edomites who became the Romans. They understood why Rome invaded the Holy Land. They were coming home! In the secret books of Zohar, all of this is documented.

My research into information hundreds of years old outlines the connections between the ancient Latin and Hebrew languages. I have transliterated Hebrew and the corresponding Latin to show the derivations:

Yeho-piter (Jehovah) → Jupiter = The Enfranchiser

Lavinum → Latinus = secret adherents (of the heart)

Kereth-Haggo → Carthage = Central City (Aeneas travelled from Jaffa to Carthage to Rome)

Tiro-yah → Troy/Troia = shout to God

Nepat-oon → Neptune = Dilating/Expanding (like the sea)

Jah-nu → Janus = Our Jehovah

Da-hu → Deu = God is enough

Rum-mul-hu → Romulus = risen before him

Rom → Remus = risen

Ro-omina → Roma = shepherd nourisher (suckled by wolves)

Romah → That which is exalted = Rome

Ragah → Rex = to stir up/agitate (king)

Asher-nator → Senator = who is to guard

Hital-yah → Italia = may you be exalted by God (Maybe this is why the Vatican is in Rome?)

In addition, all ancient Latin names were derived from ancient Hebrew.

Both the ancient *and* modern Holy Rabbis believe in the prophecy that the descendants of Esau/Edom will be the ones to rebuild the Third Temple in Jerusalem.

Research shows that between 40% to 60% of all Latinos have Hebrew DNA. Therefore, it is no wonder that so many Latin countries are relocating their Israel Embassies to Jerusalem.

Asia

King Bee, Queen Bee and *The Template of God-Mind* explain the flow of the Hebrews to parts of Asia, including Japan, India, Turkey, Afghanistan, China, and even Siberia.

China and India are very closely connected to Israel technologically and have a common enemy of Islam. China and India also use Israeli military weaponry. Tourism between these nations is very high.

But why do Jews have an interest in the Far East? Why do they have an affinity for Hinduism and Buddhism?

Remember Abraham's "gifts to the East." After Sarah passed away, he married a woman of dark skin named Keturah, with whom he had six sons. When they were grown, he gave them Hebrew spiritual information and sent them to the Asian nations. In the Torah, they are referred to as *Bnai Keturah*, which means the sons of Keturah. "Keturah" sounds similar to "Torah."

These sons went to India, Tibet, China, and all over Asia. The name *Buddha* comes from the Hebrew *B'Yehudah,* meaning "In Judah." Buddhism is very similar to Kabbalistic Judaism.

According to Kaballah and Zohar information, these Eastern religions should be re-integrated back into Judaism.

Some linguistic connections:

Brahma = Avraham

Sarasvati (wife of Brahma) = Sarah (wife of Abraham)

Shiva = Beer Sheva

King Solomon connected with the children of the East via his flying car. Solomon's name is listed in many places in Kashmir and Pakistan.

The three Magi came from the East. They knew all about what was happening via their connections to the Essenes in Israel.

The well-known Sanskrit Mantra, *Om Mani Padme Hum*, means "Oh, the Jewel of the Lotus, Oh my God within me."

Sanskrit uses a "crown" above certain letters, as does Hebrew.

Based on the "children of the East" coming from Israel, this mantra is actually from Hebrew.

In Hebrew, *Am Ani Pad M'hom* means "People, I am the path/the way from them."

The leader of Tibetan Buddhism is called the "Dalai Lama." This is similar to the Hebrew term *Yigdalai L'am,* which means "exalted ones to the people."

The more the languages, cultures, and even DNA of Asian peoples are examined, the more you see the direct links to the Lost Tribes of Israel.

Flow Chart of Creative Forces

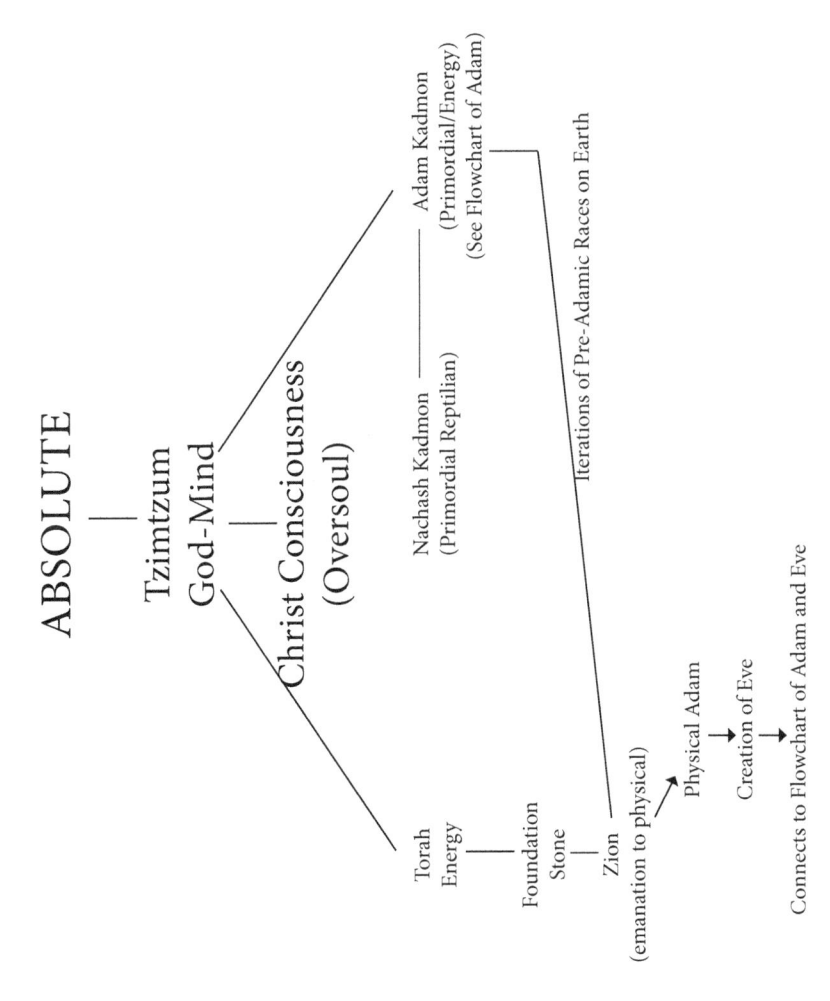

ABSOLUTE

Tzimtzum
God-Mind
Christ Consciousness
(Oversoul)

- Adam Kadmon (Primordial/Energy) (See Flowchart of Adam)
- Nachash Kadmon (Primordial Reptilian)
- Iterations of Pre-Adamic Races on Earth

Torah Energy — Foundation Stone — Zion (emanation to physical) → Physical Adam → Creation of Eve → Connects to Flowchart of Adam and Eve

Stewart A. Swerdlow • 91

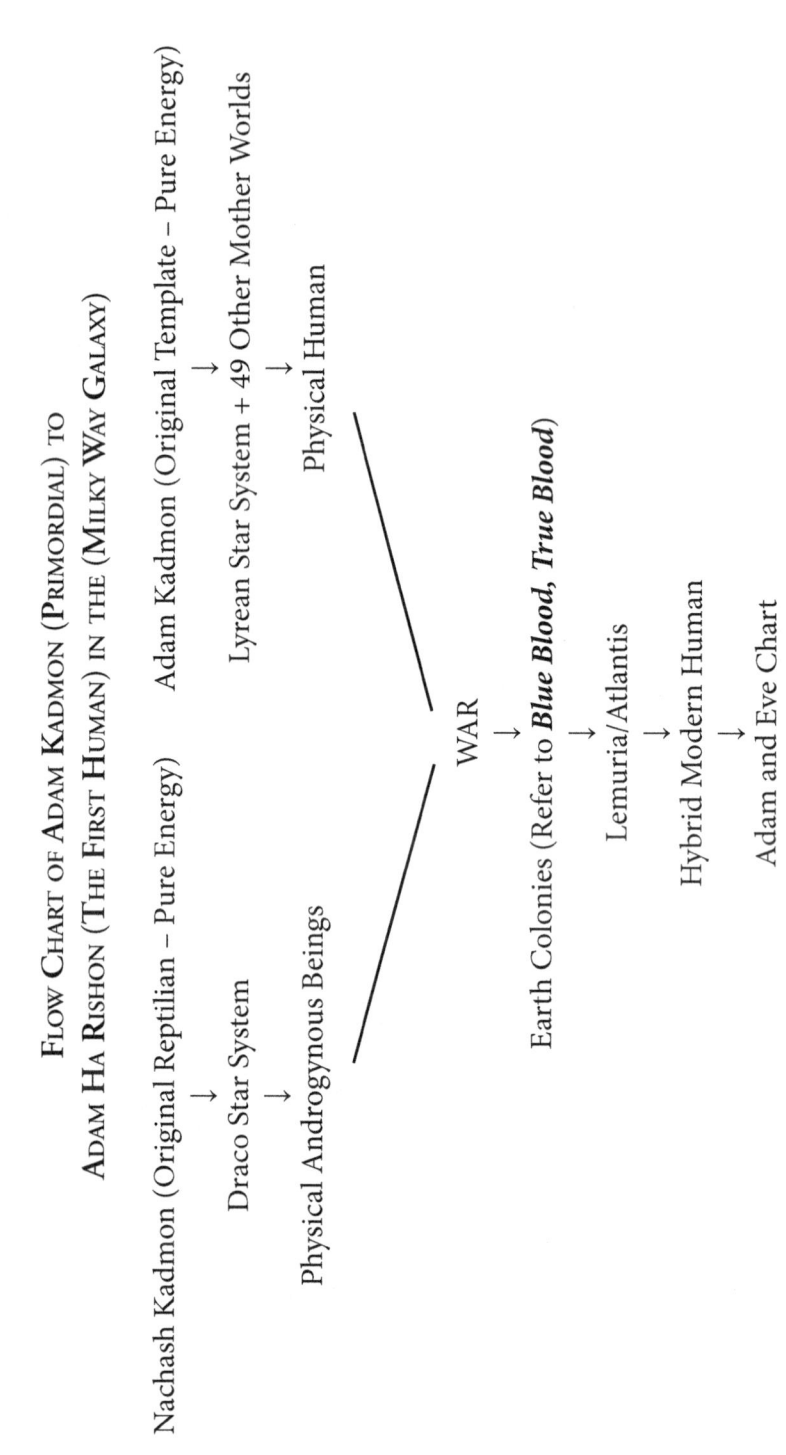

Flow Chart of Adam Kadmon (Primordial) to Adam Ha Rishon (The First Human) in the (Milky Way Galaxy)

Nachash Kadmon (Original Reptilian – Pure Energy) → Draco Star System → Physical Androgynous Beings ↘

Adam Kadmon (Original Template – Pure Energy) → Lyrean Star System + 49 Other Mother Worlds → Physical Human ↘

WAR → Earth Colonies (Refer to **Blue Blood, True Blood**) → Lemuria/Atlantis → Hybrid Modern Human → Adam and Eve Chart

Stewart A. Swerdlow • 93

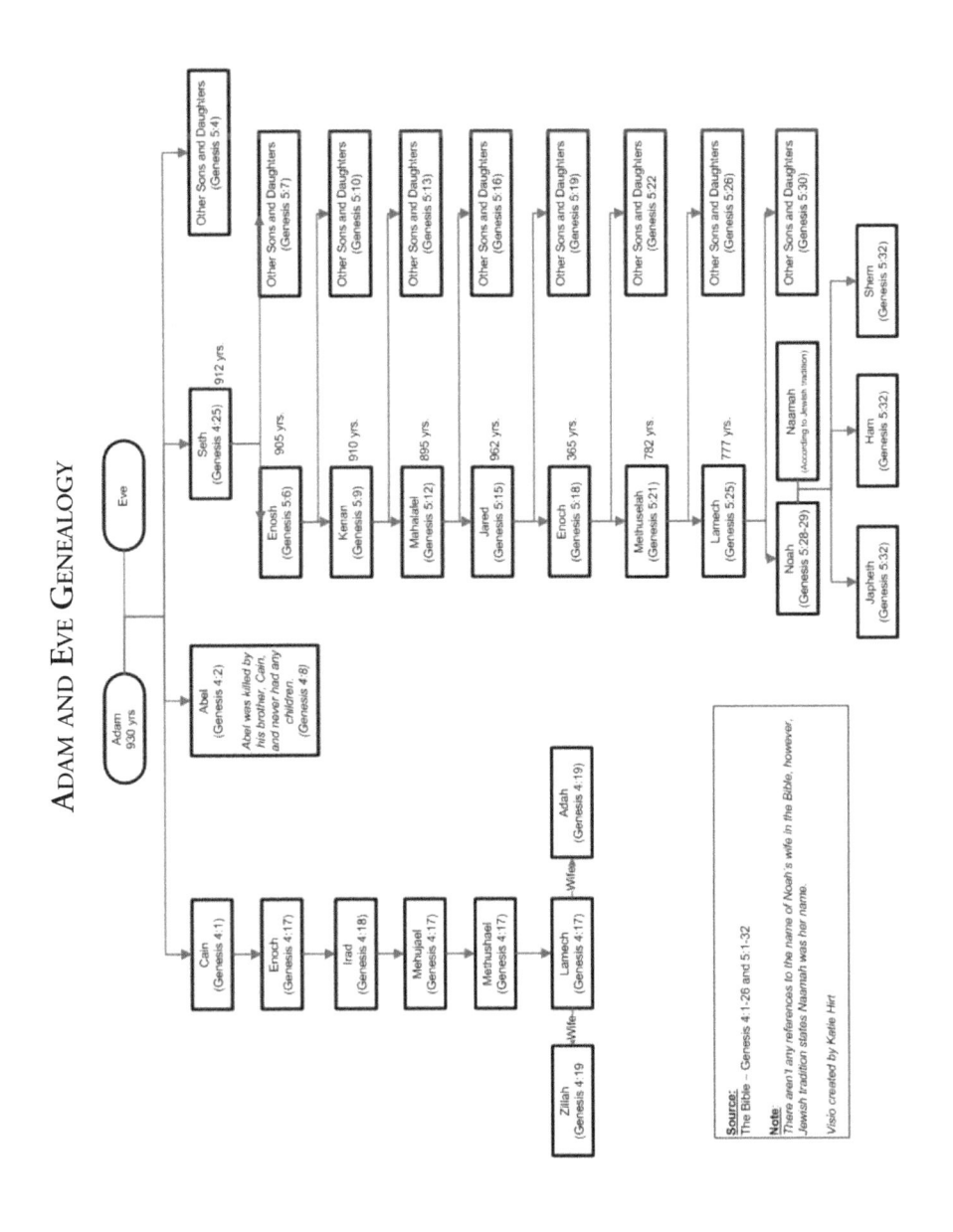

ADAM AND EVE GENEALOGY

- Adam (930 yrs)
- Eve

Line of Seth:
- Seth (Genesis 4:25) — 912 yrs
  - Other Sons and Daughters (Genesis 5:4)
- Enosh (Genesis 5:6) — 905 yrs
  - Other Sons and Daughters (Genesis 5:7)
- Kenan (Genesis 5:9) — 910 yrs
  - Other Sons and Daughters (Genesis 5:10)
- Mahalalel (Genesis 5:12) — 895 yrs
  - Other Sons and Daughters (Genesis 5:13)
- Jared (Genesis 5:15) — 962 yrs
  - Other Sons and Daughters (Genesis 5:16)
- Enoch (Genesis 5:18) — 365 yrs
  - Other Sons and Daughters (Genesis 5:19)
- Methuselah (Genesis 5:21) — 782 yrs
  - Other Sons and Daughters (Genesis 5:22)
- Lamech (Genesis 5:25) — 777 yrs
  - Other Sons and Daughters (Genesis 5:26)
- Noah (Genesis 5:28-29) — Naamah (According to Jewish tradition)
  - Other Sons and Daughters (Genesis 5:30)
  - Shem (Genesis 5:32)
  - Ham (Genesis 5:32)
  - Japheth (Genesis 5:32)

Line of Cain:
- Abel (Genesis 4:2) — Abel was killed by his brother, Cain, and never had any children. (Genesis 4:8)
- Cain (Genesis 4:1)
- Enoch (Genesis 4:17)
- Irad (Genesis 4:18)
- Mehujael (Genesis 4:17)
- Methushael (Genesis 4:17)
- Lamech (Genesis 4:17) — Wives: Zillah (Genesis 4:19), Adah (Genesis 4:19)

Source:
The Bible – Genesis 4:1-26 and 5:1-32

Note:
There aren't any references to the name of Noah's wife in the Bible, however, Jewish tradition states Naamah was her name.

Visio created by Katie Hirt

Miscellaneous Historical Facts

During my research, I discovered many interesting historical and religious facts that are challenging to fit into any one specific topic. These bullet points are a small sample of what is important for you to know.

- DNA shows that humans interbred with Neanderthals and a mystery species.

- A 2012 study showed that sub-Saharan Africans did not leave Africa. There are no African genetic markers in non-African participants.

- Humans have substantial DNA from non-Homo Sapiens species.

- Artificial hybridization is evident in human DNA.

- The priests of Ancient Egypt claimed that Atlantis existed and its first king, Poseidon, married Cleito. They had five sets of twins. The oldest boy was named Atlas, after the star in the Pleiades from which they came. Read *Blue Blood, True Blood* and *True World History* for more detailed information.

- Native Americans/Amerindians show a haplogroup in their Y-chromosomes related to Jews and Basques.

- Rh-factor attacks fetuses, proving that humans are not all descended from the same group.

- Basques, Guanches, Aztecs, Etruscans, Maya, and Welsh are all related.

- The Etruscans, Greeks, Vikings, and Cherokees all wrote or spoke about pygmies, which the Vikings called Skraelings. They were 27 in./65 cm. tall and fought giant cranes.

- Tall natives guard the entrances to the Inner Earth in the Amazon jungle and say that if you enter, you can never return. Some European expeditions have vanished in the past.

- Civilizations on Earth are much older than history states.

- There are linguistic/language commonalities in all cultures, globally.

- Catastrophes struck Earth every few thousand years—meteors, asteroids, comets, and so forth.

- The Waitahe people in New Zealand are connected culturally to the Andes, Easter Island, and Tahiti. They speak of white-skinned ancestors with red hair and beards. This was before 10,000 BC.

- The Inca, Egyptians, and Mayans all say ancient structures existed on their lands before they arrived.

- Many ancient buildings are aligned with Sirius, Orion, and Pleiades.

- There are engravings in Java from 500,000 BC.

- An intricately made floor uncovered in Oklahoma is 30,000 years old.

- Deep under the ocean, scientists have found cities, roads, artifacts, and beach sand.

- Many cultures speak of seven Sages and Tall Gods. (Lemurians?)
- Many cultures speak of the People of the Serpent/Snake People.
- Spiral symbols are found in all cultures. (Vortices/wormholes?)
- The technology that built ancient structures is not available today. Ancient cultures could bend and mold stone and build huge structures overnight.
- Elongated skulls and giant skeletons are found globally.
- Enormous data scrolls are kept hidden in Tibet, Egypt, Peru, Bolivia, Mexico, Israel, India, and the Caribbean.
- Temples and ancient buildings found globally are symbolizing formulas.
- Tribal languages globally have the same or similar words and stories.
- Many pyramids are disguised as mountains. (Bosnia/Romania).
- There are repetitive tribal stories of gods from the skies.
- Many sacred sites are connected in triangle fashion.
- Obelisks and phallic stelae mark energy spots.
- Global catastrophes are determined to have occurred in 10,800 BC, 10,500 BC, 9760 BC, 3500 BC, and 2500 BC.
- Many ancient sites have layers of construction. The oldest layers are the most perfect.
- Ancient Beings are depicted as tall, slim, powerful, and magical.
- The bodies of giants that have been unearthed have been destroyed or taken away.
- There are flood stories in almost every ancient culture.

- In Hebrew Gematria, the word for Life is *Chai* and has a numerical value of 18. Multiples of this are: 18, 36, 54, 72, 108, etc.

- The radius of the Moon in miles = 1080 (10 x 108)

- 1080 x 2 = 2160 = Great Year, the time is takes for the Sun to traverse each zodiac.

- 4 x 10,800 = The distance between Earth and Sun (From Foundation Stone).

- The atomic weight of silver = 108 (Oversoul)

- In Hebrew Gematria the value for the word for *Truth* is 72.

- The human body is 72% water.

- A pentagram has angles of 72 degrees.

- It takes 72 years for the Earth's axis to move 1 degree.

- It took 72 accomplices of Set to kill Osiris.

- There are 72 pentagrams at the base of the Washington Monument.

- There are 72 vortices on the Earth.

- There are 72 energy centers on the human body.

- In Greek the word *betylo* = the Zeus stone from heaven. Betylo comes from the Hebrew *Beth-el* meaning House of God, which was built over the Foundation Stone (from heaven).

- Ancient texts in the Zohar say that giants were created by Satan, who also created many alien races.

- Satan was an angel; *Helel* means "shining one or Lucifer."

- The story of Enoch and the Nefilim is about defiled human DNA.

- There is a technological and energetic connection between Machu Picchu, Giza, Easter Island, Puma Penku, Tiahuanaco, Lhasa, Findhorn, Bermuda Triangle, Angkor Wat, Nazca, and Stonehenge.
- Stargates are time portals and interdimensional transports.
- The Hebrew Bible speaks about the destruction of the fifth planet, which it calls Rahab/Maldek.
- Giant skeletons are found in mounds in the Midwestern and Southern USA.
- Figurines drilled with precision were found underneath layers of lava/coal over 15 million years old in Idaho, California, West Virginia, New Hampshire, Illinois, Massachusetts, and in other countries.
- Amerindian DNA is related to Egyptians and Hebrews.
- There are linguistic similarities between Cherokee, Ancient Egyptian, and Hebrew.
- CERN is actually short for Cernnunos, which is a Celtic Demon.
- Rituals and Magick are performed at CERN.
- CERN in Switzerland is the new Tower of Babel.
- North American Bigfoot DNA samples show it contains: mitochondrial human female, male nuclear DNA, and an unknown species.
- Deep State wants future humanity to consist of cyborg + AI= Nefilim DNA.
- Remnant genetics of Nefilim manifests six fingers and six toes.
- Earth has 260 trillion miles of cubic mass + 13 million cubic miles of unknown mass.

The Sicarii

Who are the Sicarii? Most people never heard of them. The Sicarri were the original assassins as explained in Wikipedia:

Sicarii—from Wikipedia, the free encyclopedia

The **Sicarii** (Modern Hebrew: סיקריים *siqari'im*) were a splinter group of the Jewish Zealots who, in the decades preceding Jerusalem's destruction in 70 CE, strongly opposed the Roman occupation of Judea and attempted to expel them and their sympathizers from the area. The Sicarii carried *sicae*, or small daggers, concealed in their cloaks. At public gatherings, they pulled out these daggers to attack Romans and Hebrew Roman sympathizers alike, blending into the crowd after the deed to escape detection.

The Sicarii are regarded as one of the earliest known organized assassination units of cloak and daggers, predating the Islamic Hashishin and Japanese ninja by centuries. The Spanish term "sicario" used in Latin America is synonymous with a hitman working for one of the various drug cartels, derives from sicarii. This is also explained in the opening of the 2015 film Sicario.

Etymology

In Latin, *Sicarii* is the plural form of *Sicarius* "dagger-man," "dagger-wielder." *Sica* here comes from the root *secor*, "to slice." In later Latin usage, "sicarius" was also the standard term for a murderer (see, e.g., the *Lex Cornelia de Sicariis et Veneficiis*), and to this day "sicario" is a salaried assassin in Spanish and a commissioned murderer in Italian. Sicário in Portuguese.

History

Victims of the Sicarii are thought to have included Jonathan the High Priest, although it is possible that his murder was orchestrated by the Roman governor Antonius Felix. Some murders were met with severe retaliation by the Romans on the entire Hebrew population of the country. However, on some occasions, the Sicarii would release their intended victim if their terms were met. Much of what is known about the Sicarii comes from the Romano-Jewish by Josephus, who wrote that the Sicarii agreed to release the kidnapped secretary of Eleazar, governor of the Temple precincts, in exchange for the release of ten captured assassins.

At the beginning of the First Roman-Jewish War, the Sicarii, and (possibly) Zealot helpers (Josephus differentiated between the two but did not explain the main differences in depth), gained access to Jerusalem and committed a series of atrocities in an attempt to incite the population into war against Rome. In one account, given in the Talmud, they destroyed the city's food supply, using starvation to force the people to fight against the Roman siege, instead of negotiating peace. Their leaders, including Menahem ben Yehuda and Eleazar ben Ya'ir, were notable figures in the war, and the group fought in many battles against the Romans as soldiers. Together with a small group of followers, Menahem made his way to the fortress of Masada, took over a Roman garrison and slaughtered all 700 soldiers there. They also took over another fortress called Antonia and overpowered the troops of Agrippa II. He also trained them to conduct various guerrilla operations on Roman convoys and legions stationed around Judea.

Josephus also wrote that the Sicarii raided nearby Hebrew villages including Ein Gedi, where they massacred 700 women and children.

The Zealots, Sicarii and other prominent rebels finally joined forces to attack and temporarily take Jerusalem from Rome in 66 AD, where they took control of the Temple in Jerusalem, executing anyone who tried to oppose their power. The local populace resisted their control and launched a series of sieges and raids to remove the rebel factions. The rebels eventually silenced the uprising and Jerusalem stayed in their hands for the duration of the war. The Romans finally came to take back the city, and they led counter-attacks and sieges to starve the rebels inside. The rebels held for some time, but the constant bickering and the lack of leadership led the groups to disintegrate. The leader of the Sicarii, Menahem, was killed by rival factions during an altercation. Soon, the Romans regained control, and finally destroyed the whole city in 70 AD.

Eleazar and his followers returned to Masada and continued their rebellion against the Romans until 73 AD. The Romans eventually took the fortress and, according to Josephus, found that most of its defenders had committed suicide rather than surrender. In Josephus' *The Jewish War* (vii), after the fall of the Temple in 70 AD, the *sicarii* became the dominant revolutionary Hebrew faction, scattered abroad. Josephus particularly associates them with the mass suicide at Masada in 73 AD and to the subsequent refusal "to submit to the taxation census when Cyrenius was sent to Judea to make one" (Josephus) as part of their rebellion's religious and political scheme.

Judas Iscariot, one of the Twelve Apostles of Jesus according to the New Testament, was believed by some to be a sicarius. This opinion is objected to by modern historians, mainly because Josephus in *The War of the Hebrews* (2:254–7) mentions the appearance of the Sicarii as a new phenomenon during the procuratorships of Felix (52–60 AD), having no apparent relation with the group called Sicarii by Romans at times of Quirinius. The 2nd century compendium of Jewish oral law, the Mishnah (*Makhshirin* 1:6), mentions the word *sikrin* (Hebrew: סיקרין), perhaps related to Sicarii, and which is explained by the early rabbinic commentators as being related to the Greek: ληστής (= robbers), and to government personnel involved with implementing the laws of Sicaricon. Maimonides, in his Mishnah Commentary (*Makhshirin* 1:6), explains the same word *sikrin* as meaning «people who harass and who are disposed to being violent.»

The Sikrikim, as mentioned in the preceding article, became the Sikhs in Asia. The Sikhs created the nation of Sikkim, which was eventually absorbed into India.

The Sicarii still exists today in another form. You may know it as the Mossad.

The Sicarii trained the ancient Arabs to be Hashashim, from which the current word derives: assassin.

The Sicarii also trained the Japanese Ninjas and Samarai. The Sicarii also became the Sikh warriors. Eventually, the Sicarii travelled with the fleeing Essenes to train the Vikings and Templars.

The Sicarii learned their trade from King Solomon's demonic army.

Sabbateans

The Sabbateans are a little known group that many think no longer exists, yet they are a major factor not only in historical events but also in current events.

From Wikipedia:

The **Sabbateans** (or **Sabbatians**) were a variety of followers of disciples and believers in Sabbatai Zevi (1626–1676), a Jewish rabbi who was proclaimed to be the Jewish Messiah in 1666 by Nathan of Gaza. Vast numbers of Jews in the Jewish diaspora accepted his claims, even after he became a Jewish apostate with his conversion to Islam in the same year. Sabbatai Zevi's followers, both during his "Messiahship" and after his conversion to Islam, are known as Sabbateans. They can be grouped into three: "Maaminim" (believers), "Haberim" (associates), and "Ba'ale Milhamah" (warriors).

Part of the Sabbateans lived on until well into the 20th century as Dönmeh.

In Jewish history many Jews after Sabbatai Zvi's apostasy, although horrified, clung to the belief that Zvi could still be regarded as the true Jewish messiah. They constituted the largest number of Sabbateans during the seventeenth and eighteenth centuries. By the nineteenth century Jewish Sabbateans had been reduced to small groups of hidden followers who feared being discovered for their beliefs that were deemed to be entirely heretical and antithetical to classical Judaism. These very Jews fell under the category of Sectarian Sabbateans which was born when many Sabbateans refused to accept that Zvi's apostasy might have been indicative of the fact that their faith was genuinely an illusion.

Another large group of Sabbateans succeeding the apostasy began to view Islam in an extremely negative light. Polemics against Islam erupted directly after Zvi's conversion. Some of these attacks were considered part of a largely Anti-Sabbatean agenda. Accusations coming from Anti-Sabbateans revolved around the idea that Sabbatai Zvi's conversion to Islam was rightfully an indicator of a false claim of messianism.

Jewish historians have stated that it is hard to describe the national sense of shock and trauma that set in when the masses of Jews all over the world learned that someone as famous as Sabbatai Zevi had officially abandoned his faith for Islam. However, the fact remains that Zevi is the most famous Jew to have become a Muslim, which is also what the term Sabbatean has come to denote. Many within Zevi's inner circle followed him into Islam, including his wife Sarah and most of his closest relatives and friends. Nathan of Gaza, the scholar closest to Zevi, who had caused Zevi to reveal his Messiahship and in turn became his prophet, never followed his master into Islam but remained a Jew, albeit excommunicated by his Jewish brethren.

Sabbatean – Sufi similarities

Claims of ties between Sabbatean Kabbalah and Sufism go back to the days of Sabbatai Zevi. This is largely based on the contention that Zevi's exile in the Balkans brought him into close contact with several forms of unorthodox Sufism which existed in the region. The Dönme community of Salonika came to play a significant role in the Sufi life of the region and its members actively involved with a number of Sufi orders, particularly the Mevlevi. Some alleged similarities between Dönme and unorthodox Sufi practice seem to exist, including the violation of *kashrut/halal*, sexual license, ecstatic singing, mystical interpretations of sacred scripture, and the practice of ritual meals. However, confirmed direct ties between Sabbatai Zevi and any Sufi order are conjectural and hearsay. The often claimed connection between the movement and Bektashi Sufism relies merely on circumstantial evidence and coincidence rather than any concrete substantiation. During Zevi's lifetime the Bektashi order had yet to attain widespread popularity in the Balkans; it came to dominate southern Albania only in the late 19th century. Nevertheless, there were a number of other heterodox Sufi movements in the region in the mid-17th century, including the Hamzevis, Melamis and Qalandars.

The Dönme

Inside the Ottoman Empire, those followers of Zevi who had converted to Islam but who secretly continued Jewish observances and Brit Mila became known as the *Dönme* (Turkish: *dönme* "convert").

The Emden-Eybeschutz controversy

The Emden-Eybeschutz controversy was a serious rabbinical disputation with wider political ramifications in Europe that followed the accusations by Rabbi Jacob Emden (1697–1776) who was a fierce opponent of the Sabbateans, against Rabbi Jonathan Eybeschutz (1690–1764) whom he accused of being a secret Sabbatean.

The Emden-Eybeschutz controversy arose concerning the amulets which Emden suspected Eybeschutz of issuing. It was alleged that these amulets recognized the messianic claims of Sabbatai Zevi. Emden then accused Eybeschutz of heresy. Emden was known for his attacks directed against the adherents, or those he supposed to be adherents, of Sabbatai Zevi. In Emden's eyes, Eybeschutz was a convicted

Sabbatean. The controversy lasted several years, continuing even after Eybeschutz's death.

Emden's assertion of heresy was chiefly based on the interpretation of some amulets prepared by Eybeschutz, in which Emden professed to see Sabbatean allusions. Hostilities began before Eybeschutz left Prague; when Eybeschutz was named chief rabbi of the three communities of Altona, Hamburg, and Wandsbek (1751), the controversy reached the stage of intense and bitter antagonism. Emden maintained that he was at first prevented by threats from publishing anything against Eybeschutz. He solemnly declared in his synagogue the writer of the amulets to be a Sabbathean heretic and deserving of *cherem* (excommunication).

The majority of the rabbis in Poland, Moravia, and Bohemia, as well as the leaders of the Three Communities, supported Eybeschutz: the accusation was "utterly incredible" - in 1725, Eybeschutz was among the Prague rabbis who excommunicated the Sabbatean sect. (Others suggest that the rabbis issued this ruling because they feared the repercussions if their leading figure was found to be a Sabbatean.

The controversy was a momentous incident in Jewish history of the period, involving both Rabbi Yechezkel Landau and the Vilna Gaon, and may be credited with having crushed the lingering belief in Sabbatai current even in some Orthodox circles. In 1760 the quarrel broke out once more when some Sabbatean elements were discovered among the students of Eybeschutz' *yeshivah*. At the same time his younger son, Wolf, presented himself as a Sabbatean prophet, with the result that the *yeshivah* was closed.

Sabbateans and early Hasidism

Some scholars see seeds of the Hasidic movement within the Sabbatean movement. When Hasidism began to spread its influence, a serious schism evolved between the Hasidic and non-Hasidic Jews. Those who rejected the Hasidic movement dubbed themselves as *misnagdim* ("opponents").

Critics of Hasidic Judaism expressed concern that Hasidism might become a messianic sect as had occurred among the followers of both Sabbatai Zevi and Jacob Frank. However *The Baal Shem Tov*, the founder of Hasidism, came at a time when the Jewish masses of Eastern Europe were reeling in bewilderment and disappointment engendered by the two Jewish false messiahs Sabbatai Zevi (1626–1676) and Jacob Frank (1726–1791) in particular.

Sabbateans and modern secularism

Some scholars have noted that the Sabbatean movement in general fostered and connected well with the principles of modern secularism. Related to this is the drive of the Donmeh in Turkey for secularizing their society just as European Jews promoted the values of Age of Enlightenment and its Jewish equivalent the *haskalah*.

Disillusioned Jewish Sabbateans

Former followers of Shabbatai do penance for their support of him.

Sabbatai's conversion to Islam was extremely disheartening for the world's Jewish communities. Among the masses of the people the greatest confusion reigned. In addition to the misery and disappointment from within, Muslims and Christians jeered at and scorned the credulous and duped Jews. In spite of Sabbatai's apostasy, many

> of his adherents still tenaciously clung to him, claiming that his conversion was a part of the Messianic scheme. This belief was further upheld and strengthened by the likes of Nathan of Gaza and Samuel Primo, who were interested in maintaining the movement

The Frankists continued on into later centuries, connected to the Rothschilds and Illuminati Satanists. Jeffrey Epstein originated via the Frankists, though he was connected to intelligence agencies for the Deep State.

As I previously wrote about the Christ figure commonly known as Jesus, he was involved in sexual ritual magick with both males and females, using that energy for his purposes.

The Sabbateans took up the rituals of Christ, and believed in orgies, drugs, alternate sexuality, wife sharing, and even pedophilia! They believed that practicing this blatant negativity exposed the mind-patterns so that they could be eliminated instead of suppressed. It is analogous to putting hot water in a dirty pot to clean it. All the junk comes to the surface first so it can be dumped, then the pot scrubbed and cleaned.

The Sabbateans also infiltrated the elites in Christianity as well as Islam during the Ottoman Empire, which allowed the Jews/Sabbateans to control the Christians and the Muslims.

All of this is now coming to fruition in Saudi Arabia, Turkey, Jordan, and other Muslim nations, in conjunction with Israel and Messianic Times.

Could all of this have been an elaborate plot to lead to control during End Times?

More Templar History Revealed

Since *True World History* and *The Template of God-Mind*, I have uncovered further important Templar information.

The Templars were the first standing army in the Western World. They developed banking, hotels/roadhouses, cathedrals, and healing centers. They venerated Mary Magdalene and were devoted to protecting the offspring of Christ and the Magdalene.

Templar building designs, symbols, secrets, and Holy artifacts are unrivaled by any other group to this day, except perhaps for the Zohar/Kabbalistic rabbis and Central/East Asian holy men. There may be a few such small groups hidden in Africa and the Andes Mountains.

There are literally thousands of books written about the Templars over the last 900 years, but most of them contain false information, accusations, suppositions, minutiae that are excruciating to read, and for the most part vast misinterpretations.

The official start of the Templars is documented in 1118 AD. But other documents have surfaced showing Templar signatures in 1111 AD in Portugal, and that they may already have existed in 1096. This makes sense, given that they were created by the Cistercian Order.

In ancient times, in Western Iberia, there was a land and a people called "Lusitania." These people came from a Celtic group who called themselves Lusitani.

Luz = hazelnut, or reference to the pineal gland.

Ani = I am.

Tan = give.

Lusitani is Hebrew for: I give my pineal gland.

On their land was a city named Porto Cale, which means beautiful harbor. Porto Cale was named after the Gaelic/Celtic goddess Cailleach.

Since the Celts were descended from Atlantean refugees and the Hebrew Tribes migrated west to the Atlantic area, it is highly likely that they would have mixed to create this new people.

In Hebrew, *Cal* = all, *Ach* = brothers. *Calilleach* = All Brothers.

However, since this was the name of a goddess, it may be from the Hebrew *Cal Achot* = All sisters.

Nearby was an important town named Braga. This name comes from the Hebrew word *Bracha*, meaning blessings.

It was in Braga that many treaties were signed between the Templars and Contesa Tareja, who was in charge of the land. She seemed to know that the Templars needed this location for their work and safety. In return, the Templars helped rid the region of Muslim invaders as well as to help the Contesa gain complete control of this land from her family in Castille.

The Template of God-Mind describes how the Essenes evolved into Viking priests, then moved to Burgundy/Champagne, known as the Twin Kingdoms in what is now France. There, the Templars began the Cistercian Order.

All of the European inhabitants of Western Iberia originated from emigrants from Burgundy and Champagne. The name Burgundy is derived after a Celtic Tribe in Denmark/Danmark called the Burgundii. Remember, Denmark now owns the Island of Barnholm where the Cistercians originated.

In Hebrew:

Burgundy → *B'or Gan Eden* = In the light of the Garden of Eden.

This is a reference to Adam and his descendants who became Essenes, developed Christ, and then the Templars.

When the Templars were asked to go to Iberia to fight the Muslims, they united with The Order of Sion of Jerusalem. The Order of Sion of Jerusalem was founded in ancient times around the time of the Essenes to fight the Romans along with the Sicarri.

In Braga, Count Dom Henrique and his family signed land over to the Templars in accordance with the desires of his mother, Countess Tareja. The Templars built large castles and monasteries with vast underground tunnels and caverns that went on for many kilometers.

According to some of the documents signed by the Knights in Braga on behalf of their Order, there may have been 11 knights. In the Cistercian Chronicles that have been saved in old libraries, they named Count Hughes de Payns, Godefroi de Bouillon, plus nine other knights, for a total of 11 knights! Could there actually have been 13? That would make sense.

In the northwest of what is now Spain, just above the city of Braga, there is a city named Gijon. The ancient Hebrew name for the Nile River was….Gihon!

The Iberian/Portuguese royalty all originated in the Twin Kingdoms of Burgundy/Champagne. Champagne, as well as Burgundy, has Hebrew origins.

Champagne → *Shem B'gan* = Name (of God) in the garden (of Eden).

The capital city of Portugal is Lisbon. In Portuguese, Lisboa.

Lisboa → *L'ish Bo* = To the man who comes.

As the Templars were given more and more land by the Countess and her son, they actually consolidated these lands under the jurisdiction of the donating family. This created the first Nation State in Europe, Portugal, under Templar authority. It was because of this that in 1307, when the King of France, the Pope, and their allies, attacked and jailed the Templars in Europe, the Templars were given safe haven in Portugal. In Portugal they changed their names to "The Knights of Christ."

The Order of Cister/Cistercians make their new members take a vow to "protect the bloodline of David." This refers to the children of Christ and Mary Magdalene. All the documents are signed with the "hooked X," as explained in *The Template of God-Mind*.

The name Portugal has several layers of meanings.

Port o Cale = Port of Calleach

Port du Gaul = Port of France/Gaul

Por Tu Gral = Through you, the Grail (this one is likely the most accurate)

The Templars were accused by King Phillip IV of worshipping Baphomet. Baphomet was not a demon, as misinterpreted by researchers and New Age authors.

In Arabic, the Muslims referred to Mohammed as *Abu Fihamet* meaning "Father of Wisdom." In the Middle Ages, the ignorant French peasants and priests pronounced Abu Fihamet as "Baphomet" when referring to Mohammed.

The Templars were in possession of the Shroud of Turin, which has the electromagnetically created image of Christ embedded in the linens. During secret prayer services, the Templars prayed in front of this artifact. King Phillip's spies, who infiltrated the Templars in order to find evidence of blasphemy for conviction, saw this ceremony and reported it as worshipping Mohammed, which they called "Baphomet."

Thus began the false accusations that the Templars actually despised Christ and made the Knights spit on the cross. In actuality, they used ribbons or threads to kiss the shroud.

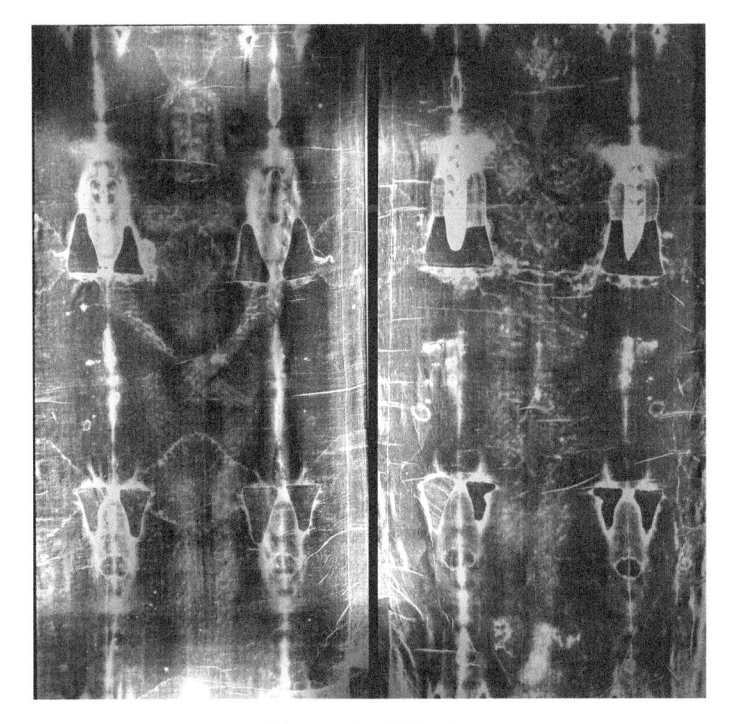

Shroud of Turin

After the horrendous arrests, persecutions, tortures, abuse, and executions, the surviving Templars changed their names, fled, or went into hiding. It was only in Scotland under the Bruce and Sinclair families, and in Portugal, as The Knights of Christ, that the Templars continue on to this day.

Interestingly, the Portuguese Knights of Christ connected frequently to the Coptic Christians in Ethiopia, where the Ark of the Covenant was being kept in secret.

In summary, the Essenes/Vikings/Cistercians/Templars created a country, Portugal, to hide the descendants of King David and move them to North America, as well as Brazil.

Map of Iberia

Map of Portugal

Vikings/Hebrews

Viking priests and Viking belief systems were derived from the Lost Tribes of Israel who migrated to Scandinavia after the Roman destruction of the Second Temple.

Even to the Vikings, there were variations in the faith depending on where they lived. Some of the Vikings began converting to Christianity after exploring and raiding the coast of England and France. Toward the end of the Viking age, almost everyone in Scandinavia was a Christian.

In Iceland people tend to call the Viking religion Ásatrú; in Denmark, they also call it Ásatrú or Ásatrú and Vanatrú, Some people in the USA even call it Odinism. Odinism sounds like you believe or pray to one God but Ásatrú is not just about one God.

Norse/Viking core beliefs are outlined below. At the end, compare Hebrew Sefirot/Tree of Life to the Viking Yggdrasil.

The Nine Worlds in Norse Mythology
www. norsemythology.org

There are nine worlds in Norse Mythology; they are called Niflheim, Muspelheim, Asgard, Midgard, Jotunheim, Vanaheim, Alfheim, Svartalfheim, Helheim. The nine worlds in Norse mythology are held in the branches and roots of the world tree Yggdrasil. These realms are the home of different kind of beings, like the home of the Gods and Goddesses or giants.

Niflheim: The World of Fog and Mist

Niflheim (Old Norse: "Niðavellir") and it means ("Mist home" or "Mist World") is the darkest and coldest region in the world according to Norse mythology. Niflheim is the first of the nine worlds and Niflheim is placed in the northern region of Ginnungagap. The eldest of the three wells are located in Niflheim which is called Hvergelmir "bubbling boiling spring" and it is protected by the huge dragon called Nidhug (Níðhöggr).

It is said that all cold rivers come from the well called Hvergelmir, and it is said to be the source of the eleven rivers in Norse mythology. The well Hvergelmir is the origin of all living and the place where every living being will go back. Elivagar "ice waves" are the rivers that existed in Niflheim at the beginning of the world. They were the streams floating out of Hvergelmir. The water from Elivagar flowed down the mountains to the plains of Ginnungagap, where it solidified to frost and ice, which gradually formed a very dense layer. This is the reason that it is very cold in the northern plains. As the world tree Yggdrasil started to grow, it stretched one of its three large roots far into Niflheim and drew water from the spring Hvergelmir.

Muspelheim: The Land of Fire

Muspelheim (Old Norse: "Múspellsheimr") was created far to the south of the world in Norse mythology. Muspelheim is a burning hot place, filled with lava, flames, sparks, and soot. Muspelheim is the home of the fire giants, fire demons and ruled by the giant Surtr. He is a sworn enemy of the Aesir. Surtr will ride out with his flaming sword in his hand at Ragnarok "Ragnarök" "the end of the world" Surtr will then attack Asgard, "the home of the Gods" and turn it into a flaming inferno.

Asgard: Home of the Gods

In the middle of the world, high up in the sky is Asgard (Old Norse: "Ásgarðr"). It's the home of the Gods and Goddesses. The male Gods in Asgard, are called Aesir, and the female Gods are called Asynjur. Odin is the ruler of Asgard and the chief of the Aesir. Odin is married to Frigg; and she is the Queen of the Aesir. Inside the gates of Asgard is Valhalla; it's the place where half of the Vikings "Einherjer" that died in battle will go for the afterlife, the other half goes to Fólkvangr.

Midgard: Home of the Humans

Midgard (Old Norse: "Miðgarðr") "middle earth" is located in the middle of the world, below Asgard. Midgard and Asgard are connected by Bifrost the Rainbow Bridge. Midgard is surrounded by a huge ocean that is impassable.

The Ocean is occupied by a huge sea serpent, the Midgard Serpent. The Midgard serpent is so huge that it encircles the world entirely, and biting its own tail. Odin and his two brothers Vili and Ve created the humans from an Ash log, the man and from an elm log, the woman.

Jotunheim: Home of the Giants

Jotunheim (Old Norse: "Jötunheimr or Útgarðr") is the home of the giants (also called Jotuns). They are the sworn enemies of the Aesir. Jotunheim consists mostly of rocks, wilderness, and dense forests, and it lies in the snowy regions on the outermost shores of the ocean. Because of this, the giants live mostly from the fish from the rivers, and the animals from the forest, because there is no fertile land in Jotunheim.

The giants and the Aesir are constantly fighting, but it also happens from time to time, that love affairs will occur.

Odin, Thor and a few others, had lovers who were giants. Loki also came from Jotunheim, but he was accepted by the Aesir and lived in Asgard. Jotunheim is separated from Asgard by the river Iving, which never freezes over. Mimir's well of wisdom is in Jotunheim, beneath the Midgard root of the ash tree Yggdrasil. The stronghold of Utgard is so big that it is hard to see the top of it. And there the feared Jotun king Utgard-Loki lives. Utgard is carved from blocks of snow and glistening icicles.

Vanaheim: Home of the Vanir

Vanaheim (Old Norse: "Vanaheimr") is the home of the Vanir Gods. The Vanir Gods is an old branch of Gods. The Vanir are masters of sorcery and magic. They are also widely acknowledged for their talent to predict the future. Nobody knows where exactly the land, Vanaheim is located, or even how it looks like. When the war between the Aesir and the Vanir ended, three of the Vanir came to live in Asgard, Njord and his children Freya and Freyr.

Alfheim: Home of the Light Elves

Alfheim (Old Norse: "Álfheimr or Ljósálfheimr") is right next to Asgard in the heaven. The light elves are beautiful creatures. They are considered the "guardian angels" The God Freyr, is the ruler of Alfheim. The Light elves are minor Gods of nature and fertility; they can help or hinder humans with their knowledge of magical powers. They also often delivered an inspiration to art or music.

Svartalfheim: Home of the Dwarves

Svartalfheim (Old Norse: "Niðavellir or Svartálfaheimr") is the home of the dwarves; they live under the rocks, in caves and underground. Hreidmar was the king of

Svartalfheim, Svartalfheim means Dark fields. The dwarves are masters of craftsmanship. The Gods of Asgard have received many powerful gifts. Like, the magical ring Draupnir and also Gungnir, Odin's spear.

Helheim: Home of the dishonorable dead

This is where all the dishonorable dead, thieves, murderers and those the Gods and Goddesses feel is not brave enough to go to Valhalla or Folkvangr. Helheim is ruled by Hel, Helheim is a very grim and cold place, and any person who arrives here will never feel joy and happiness again. Hel will use all the dead in her realm at Ragnarök to attack the Gods and Goddesses, which will be the end of the world.

In the middle of Asgard, where the Gods and Goddesses live, is Yggdrasil. Yggdrasil is the tree of life, and it is an eternal green Ash tree; the branches stretch out over all of the nine worlds in Norse mythology, and extend up and above the heavens. Yggdrasil is carried by three enormous roots, the first root from Yggdrasil is in Asgard, the home of the Gods it is just next to the well-named Urd, this is where the Gods and Goddesses have their daily meetings.

The second root from Yggdrasil goes all the way down to Jotunheim, the land of the giants, next to this root is Mimir's well. The third root from Yggdrasil goes down to Niflheim, close to the well Hvergelmir. It is here the dragon Nidhug is chewing on one of Yggdrasil's roots. Nidhug is also known to suck the blood out of the dead bodies that arrives at Hel. At the very top of Yggdrasil lives an eagle, the eagle and the dragon Nidhug are bitter enemies, and they truly despise each other. There is a squirrel named Ratatosk, and he spending almost the entire day, by running up and down the ash tree.

Ratatosk does whatever he can, to keep the hatred between the eagle and the dragon alive. Every time Nidhug says a curse or an insult about the eagle, Ratatosk will run up to the top of the tree, and tell the eagle what Nidhug just said. The eagle is equally rude in his comments about Nidhug. Ratatosk just loves to gossip, which is the reason why the eagle and the dragon remain constant foes.

What is Ragnarok?

The Vikings believed that one day the world as we know it would come to an end, they called this day for Ragnarok, (old Norse Ragnarökr). Ragnarok is not only the doom of man but also the end of the Gods and Goddesses. It will be the final battle between the Aesir and Giants. The battle will take place on the plains called Vigrid.

It is here that the mighty Midgard serpent will be emerging from the sea, while it splashes its tail and sprays poison in all directions, causing huge waves crashing towards the land. Meanwhile, the fire giant Surtr will set Asgard (the home of the Gods and Goddesses) and the rainbow bridge Bifrost on fire. The Fenrir wolf will break free of his chains and spread death and destruction. The sun and the moon will be swallowed by the wolves Sköll and Hati, and even the world tree Yggdrasil will shake the ground.

Odin will die at Ragnarok

Odin and the Fenrir wolf will fight each other to the death And Loki will turn on the Aesir, and fight Heimdall, and they will kill each other. Tyr will fight the watchdog "Garm" that guards the gates of Hel, will also kill each other.

Who kills Thor at Ragnarok?

Thor will fight the Midgard Serpent and kill it, but he will die of the poisonous wounds left behind by the Midgard Serpent. Freyr will be killed by the fire giant named Surtr. Finally, Surtr will set all the nine worlds on fire and everything sinks into the boiling sea. There is nothing the Gods can do to prevent Ragnarok. Odin's only comfort is that he can predict that Ragnarok, will not be the end of the world.

The signs of Ragnarok

There will be some warning signs if Ragnarok "the end of the world" is coming. The first sign is the murder of the God Baldr, the son of Odin and Frigg, which has already happened.

The second sign will be three uninterrupted long cold winters that will last for three years with no summer in between. The name of these uninterrupted winters are called "Fimbulwinter" during these three long years, the world will be plagued by wars, and brothers will kill brothers. The third sign will be the two wolves in the sky swallowing the sun and the moon, and even the stars will disappear and send the world into a great darkness.

How does Ragnarok begin?

A beautiful red rooster "Fjalar" which name means the "All knower," will warn all the giants that the beginning of Ragnarok has begun. At the same time in Hel, will a red rooster warn all the dishonorable dead, that the war has begun. And also in Asgard, will a red rooster "Gullinkambi" warn all the Gods.

Heimdall will blow his horn as loud as he can and that will be the warning for all the einherjar in Valhalla that the war has started. This will be the battle to end all battles, and this will be the day that all the Vikings "Einherjar" from Valhalla and Folkvangr who had died honorably in battle, to pick up their swords and armor to fight side by side with the Aesir against the Giants.

The Gods, Baldr, and Hod will be returned from the dead, to fight one last time with their brothers and sisters. Odin will be riding on his horse Sleipnir with his eagle helmet equipped and his spear Gungnir in his hand, and lead the enormous army of Asgard with all the Gods and brave einherjar to the battleground in the fields of Vigrid.

The Giants will together with Hel, and all her dishonorable dead, sail in the ship Naglfar, which is made from the fingernails of all the dead, sail to the plains of Vigrid. The dragon Nidhug will come flying over the battlefield and gather as many corpses for his never-ending hunger.

A new earth rises from the sea

When most of the Gods had perished in the mutual destruction with the Giants, it is predetermined that a new world will rise up from the water, beautiful and green. Before the battle of Ragnarok, two people, Lif "a woman" and Liftraser "a man," will find shelter in the sacred tree Yggdrasil. And when the battle is over, they will come out and repopulate the earth again.

Which gods survive Ragnarok?

Several of the Gods will survive, among them Odin's sons Vidar and Vali and his brother Honir. Thor's sons Modi and Magni will inherit their father's hammer Mjölnir.

The few Gods who survive will go to Idavoll, which has remained untouched. And here they will build new houses, the greatest of the houses will be Gimli, and will have a roof of gold. There is also a new place called Brimir, at a place called Okolnir "Never cold." It is in the mountains of Nidafjoll.

But there is also a terrible place, a great hall on Nastrond, the shore of corpses. All its doors face north to greet the screaming winds. The walls will be made of writhing snakes that pour their venom into a river that flows through the hall. This will be the new underground, full of thieves and murderers, and when they die the great dragon Nidhug, is there to feed upon their corpses.

In Norse mythology, **Mjölnir** (/ˈmjɔːlnɪər/; Old Norse: *Mjǫllnir*, IPA: [ˈmjɔlːnir]) is the hammer of Thor, the Norse god associated with thunder. Mjölnir is depicted in Norse mythology as one of the most fearsome and powerful weapons in existence, capable of leveling mountains. In its account of Norse mythology, the *Prose Edda* relates how the hammer's characteristically short handle was due to a mistake during its manufacture. Similar hammers, such as Ukonvasara, were a common symbol of the god of thunder in other North European mythologies.

Old Norse *Mjǫllnir* [ˈmjɔlːnir] regularly becomes *Mjøllnir* [ˈmjœlːnir] in Old Icelandic by the 13th century. The modern Icelandic form is *Mjölnir*, Norwegian and Danish *Mjølner*, Swedish *Mjölner*.

The name is derived from a Proto-Germanic form **meldunjaz*, from the Germanic root of **malanan* "to grind" (**melwan*, Old Icelandic *meldr*, *mjǫll*, *mjǫl* "meal, flour"), yielding an interpretation of "the grinder; crusher."

Ásgarð: the Garden of the Æsir and Ásynjur

Miðgarð: the Middle Garden, where humanity resides

Álfheim: Home of the Álfar, a race of light and dark skinned elves

Jötunheim: Home of the Jötnar, a race of mountain-giants

Vanaheim: Home of the Vanir, a race of nature-deities

Hel: the Underworld, where those who died of old age/sickness reside

Sökkdalir: the Sunken Dales, abode of the Eldjötnar, fire-giants

Niflhel, the Mist Concealed, abode of the Hrimthusar, the frost-giants

Ginnungagap: the Gaping Void, a primordial space

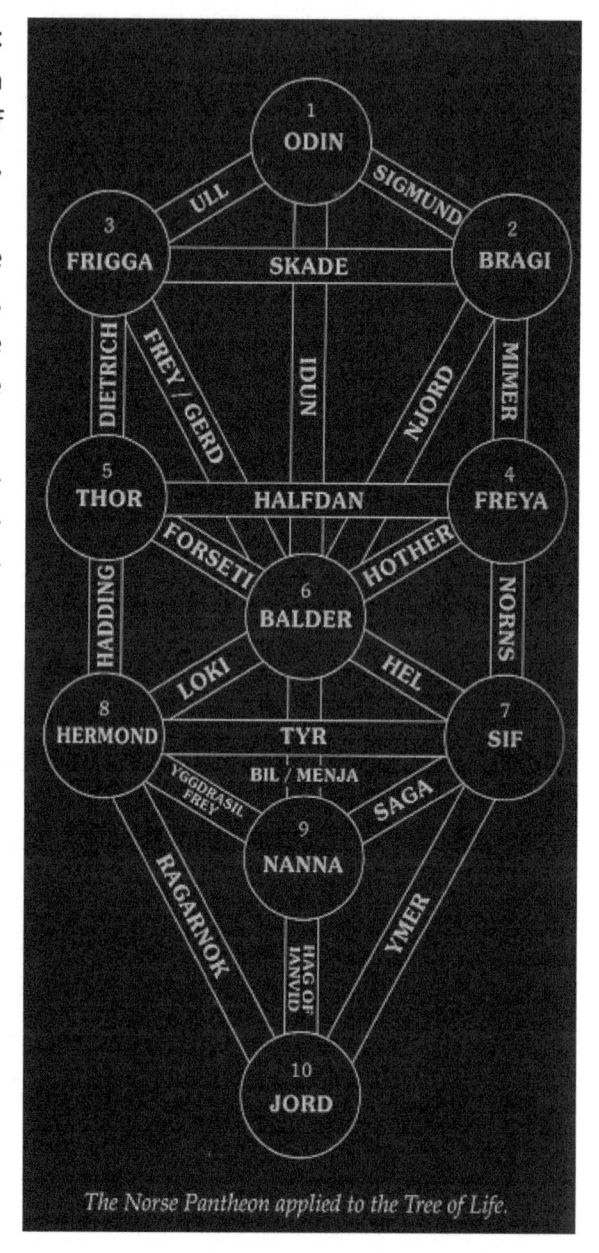

The Norse Pantheon applied to the Tree of Life.

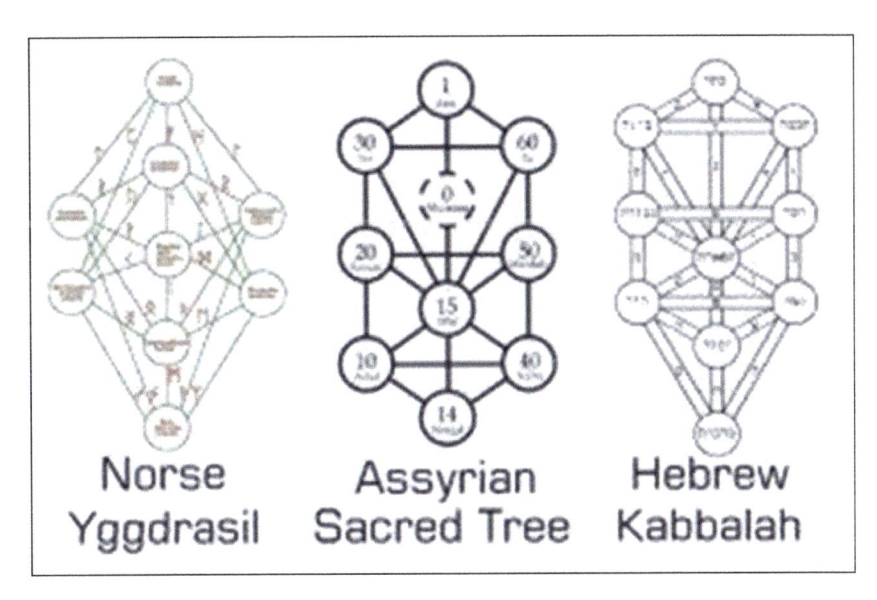

Stewart A. Swerdlow • 127

Norse Yggdrasil | **Assyrian Sacred Tree** | **Hebrew Kabbalah**

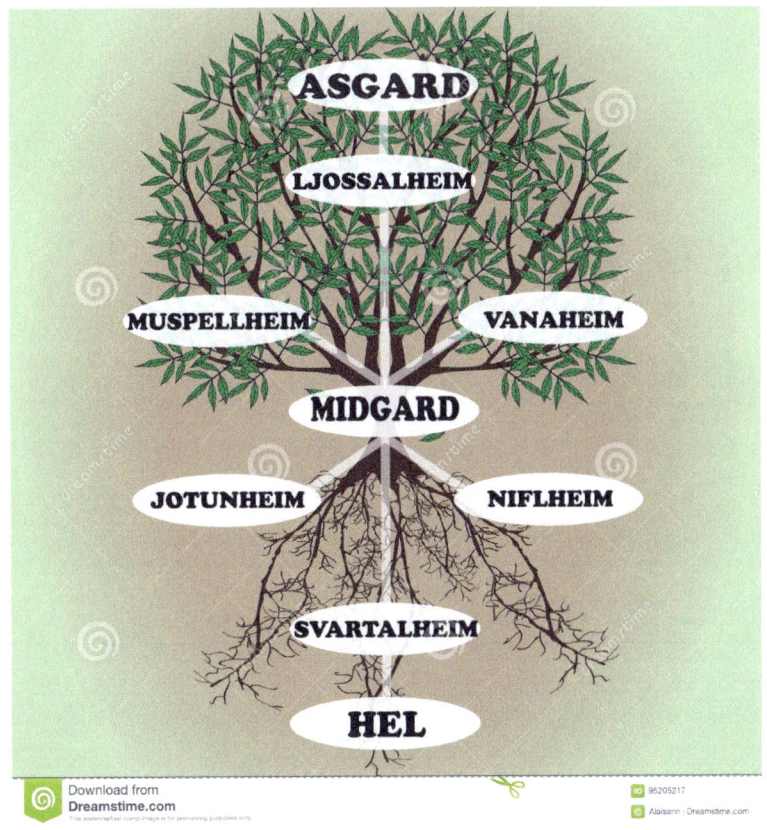

ASGARD
LJOSSALHEIM
MUSPELLHEIM — VANAHEIM
MIDGARD
JOTUNHEIM — NIFLHEIM
SVARTALHEIM
HEL

The Midgard Serpent is analogous to the Hebrew Leviathan.

The origin of the Norse name *Yggdrasil* comes from the Hebrew words *Yigdal Rosh El*, meaning "Exalted Head of God."

The final battle between Aesir and the Giants = End Times in the Bible.

Norse God *Baldr* = Baal

Thor's Hammer *Mjolnir* comes from the Hebrew words *M'yah L'nor*, meaning "From God to Light"

The Viking religion, called *Asatru*, comes from the Hebrew words *Ash Ha teru*, meaning "Fire the alarm/war cry.'

You can't make this up!

Section 3
God

God

The Sefirot are the inception or foundation for the template of all Beings, including Humankind. They are referred to in the Kabballah and Zohar as "Adam Kadmon" meaning "Primordial Man."

Sefirot

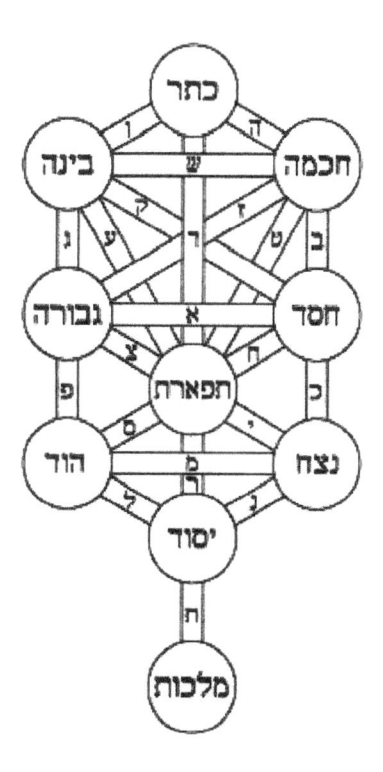

In this case, "Man" refers to the Androgynous spiritual/nonphysical "Adam" that existed before physicality. Once the physical was established, this becomes "Adam HaRishon" meaning "First Man."

Superimposing the Sefirot of the Primordial Adam upon your own Chakra System resets your structure to create healing and positive changes that bring all of your body and energy systems back to what the original design was meant to be.

When you think of the idea of Creation emanating out of the Absolute, visualize a Self-perpetuating toroid energy constantly moving forward and manifesting in all realities. In Kaballah, it is said that this is how the Hebrew alphabet/letters were created.

The Hebrew letters are numbers and are used to create spiritual formulas that can manifest in any reality, if you understand the meanings and how to use them. Only two Hebrew letters create portals that are considered to be Torah Toroids. They are the letters Mem and Samech.

Two forms of Mem

Samech

Observe how they can create a tunnel or pathway, like a vortex or wormhole.

The value of Mem in Gematria = 40. It represents nonphysical space.

The value of Samech = 60, and symbolizes inner space.

A perfect combination!

In addition, the numerical value of Member plays a significant role in history.

Noah saw it rain for 40 days and nights.

Moses led the Children of Israel for 40 years in the desert.

Jesus spent 40 days in the wilderness fighting Satan.

You must be 40 years old to study Kaballah.

Lent is 40 days long.

That number represents that each of these stories and events is a vortex that leads you to another layer of understanding the God-Mind.

Mem is also the first letter of Metatron, Moses, and Moshiach/Messiah.

Keep in mind that Metatron is not an angel or archangel. Metatron is a formula!

The first letter of the Hebrew alphabet is Aleph.

א

Aleph has the value of 1.

Aleph in Hebrew letters is spelled like this:

אָלֶף

Now, same spelling with one vowel change, and we get the word. Eleph, which stands for the number, 1000.

אֶלֶף

This is very significant when you consider the Messianic Numerical Code for the function of 999:

$$1000 - 1 = 999$$

In Kaballah there is a Messianic outline that requires 999 steps, both positive and negative, that leads to the last step, 1000, where the Moshiach ben David, the final Messiah, appears on the world.

Talmud: Represents the six orders of Mishnah.

Mishnah: Body and codex of the Oral Torah + Gemara

Gemara: Amplification and commentary of the Mishnah.

Midrash: Ancient commentary on Hebrew Scriptures.

The Kaballah is concealed within the Aggadata, which is the nonlegal aspect of Talmud. Confused yet? Jewish terms and legal aspects can be overwhelming. Study the Glossary at the end of this book!

I must give you warnings from the Holy Rabbis of ancient times. According to them:

It is forbidden to study Kaballah unless you are 40 years old and have a stomach full of meat and wine. (Red wine, I hope!)

or...

You must be at least 20 years old, married, and versed in Talmud. You must also "see" your world/life in your lifetime. What does *that* mean? How do you see your life in your lifetime?

By ***knowing*** who and what you are and by ***knowing*** the Absolute!

There is no doubt, no confusion. Only ***knowing***!

Kabbalistic Laws and Rules

The Law of Polarity

You cannot know something without contrasting to the opposite. This is why evil exists and why bad things happen. These opposites are two sides of the same coin. A Mobius Strip is a great example of this.

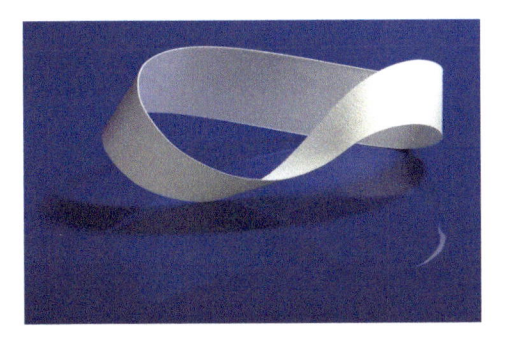

Demonstrations of polarities:

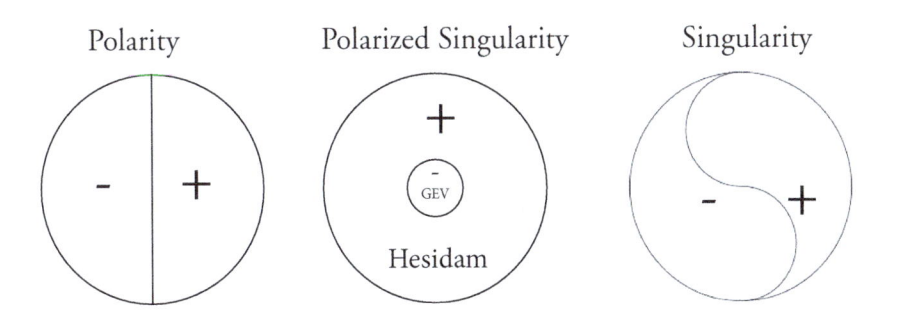

Polarity — Polarized Singularity — Singularity

(- | +) (+ / GEV / Hesidam) (- / +)

Sefirot, Chesed, and Gevurah

Chesed/Hesed is the male, positive energy that represents kindness and love.

Gevurah is the female, negative energy that represents strength and manifesting into the physical.

Both Chesed/Hesed/male/positive and Gevurah/female/negative are needed and work together.

The Kaballah formula is described in an anagram.

Chesed/Hesed=H

And in Hebrew=u

Gevurah=G

Therefore, the statement of the balance and polarity needed for existence is written as: HuG.

The "H" in "HuG" is pronounced with a hard "ch" like the German Ach.

Zohar: Five Aspects To All Creation

All things have two aspects—Chesed (M+) and Gevurah (F-)

Any aspect of HuG can be divided further into +/- (like Homeopathy)

The Chesadim(+) and Gevurot (-) mutually create each other.

HuG define each other.

HuG convert into each other (like hormones)

Zugots

All is created in paired units called Zugot. Zugots are not opposites Zugots are pairs/twins.

YHVH/male = cosmic code/fractal formula that identifies all aspects.

Adonoy/female = the physical manifestation of the fractal codes.

Weaving, as discussed in *The Template of God-Mind*, creates the unification formula:

Y-A-H-D-V-N-H-Y

The Seven Rectifications of the Decoder (Hidden Information) in Preparation for Redemption

Egalitarianism: personal and ethical conduct; overcoming negativity.

Transcendence: higher consciousness/power of Metatron= collective Oversoul of Moshiach ben Joseph.

Holism: Yesod - contains all other Sefirot. Devine attribute of Zion. All of Israel responsible for each other.

Sanctification: highest root and source of divine purity emanating from Da'at (pineal gland) and goes to vov (spinal cord).

Creativity: new aspects revealed in Formula 999 in Yesod. Advanced new Torah understandings/your unique mission.

Power: overpowering evil. Remove impurity and moral decay.

Fusion: of masculine and feminine aspects of Divinity. (HuG)

Flow Chart of Absolute Into Creation

Absolute → Tzimtzum

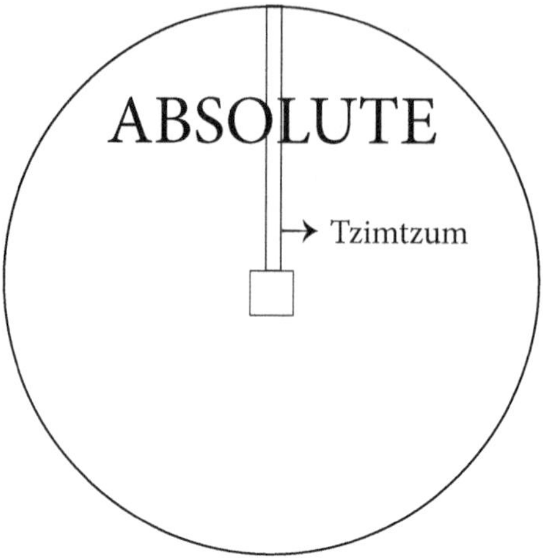

Prayer

Prayer is a function of the Left Brain and conscious/logical mind. The idea of prayer may imply "lack" and "need," hence, you are asking for something.

In Kabballah, the question is asked, "Who is praying to whom?"

Since we are all aspects of the same God-Mind, One Being, then how can anyone pray to another?

The answer is that you actually pray/send energies to another aspect of Self.

Prayers work because you are creating an affirmation for your Self.

The totality of the God-Mind/SELF enhances this and brings it to fruition.

Number 7 in Creation

The number 7 is prevalent in Creation. For example, there are:

7 days per week

7 chakras

7 pre-Adamic civilizations

7 continents on Earth

7 lower Sephirot

The 7 lower Sephirot are related to physical reality, so this is the key to the importance to the Number 7 in Creation. Number 7 means Completion.

This leaves 3 Sephirot, which are nonphysical/spiritual. The Number 3 means Perfection/Creation. For this, we look to the Sephirot.

In total, there are 10 Sephirot.

We are Divine beings, united with God eternally.

The Kabballah and Zohar give this definition of the Torah:

> ***Virtual brain through which the Absolute processes Its thoughts and expressions; the Blueprint of all Creation. Its verses, words, and letters create the consciousness through which all reality evolves and guides itself.***

The Absolute is also known as *Ain Sof*, meaning "without end." Because All is created in pairs, there are two Torahs:

Oral Torah/Written Torah, also known as Twin Torahs.

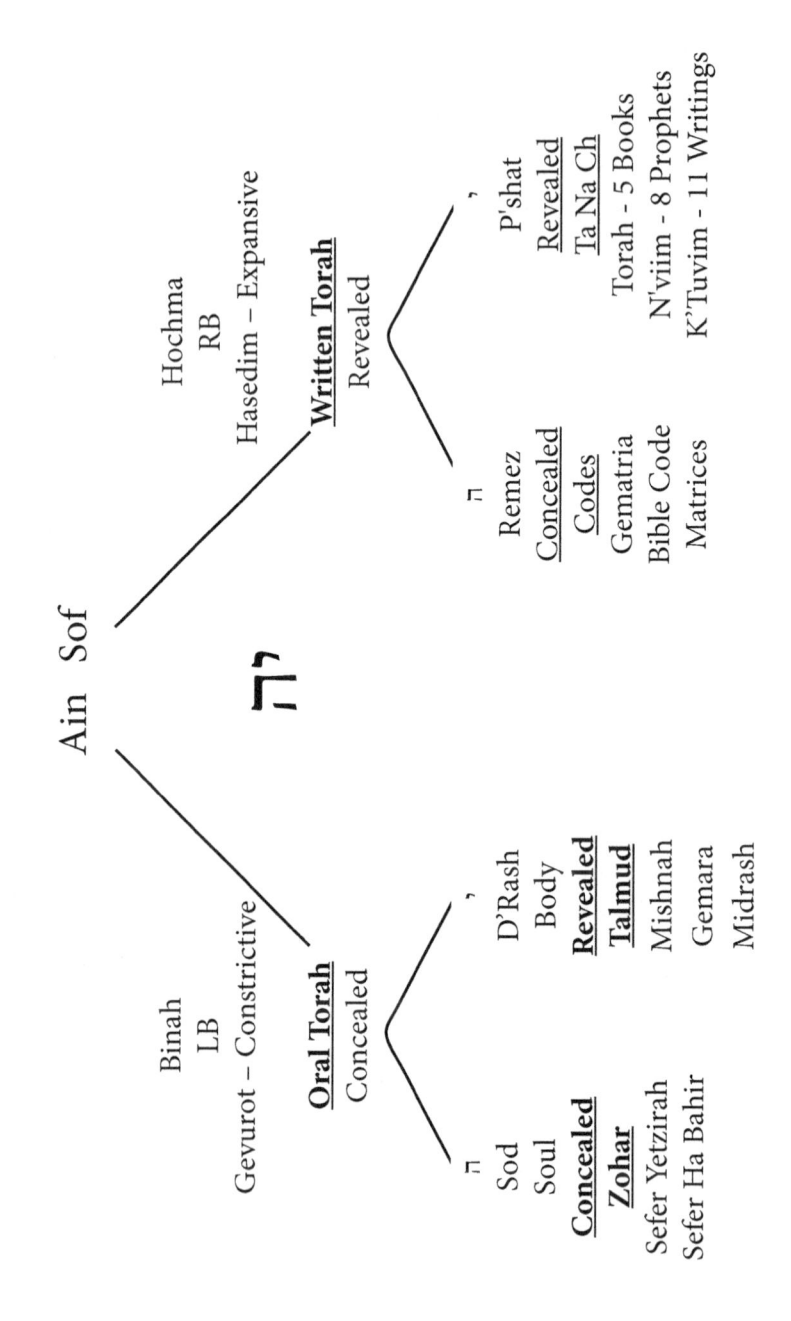

Ain Sof and Twin Torahs

Ain Sof

ה

Written Torah — Revealed

Hochma
RB
Hasedim – Expansive

ו
P'shat
Revealed
Ta Na Ch
Torah - 5 Books
N'viim - 8 Prophets
K'Tuvim - 11 Writings

י
Remez
Concealed
Codes
Gematria
Bible Code
Matrices

Oral Torah — Concealed

Binah
LB
Gevurot – Constrictive

ו
D'Rash
Body
Revealed
Talmud
Mishnah
Gemara
Midrash

ה
Sod
Soul
Concealed
Zohar
Sefer Yetzirah
Sefer Ha Bahir

Sha'ashu'a, The Secret of God's Delight

Sha'ashu'a is the basis for everything; it is the explanation of what came *before* Creation. When understood, Sha'ashu'a explains more than you can imagine.

There is a linguistic connection between the name *Yehoshua* and the Kabballah term *Sha'ashu'a*.

Yehoshua means "the God who brings salvation"

Sha'ashu'a means "God's Delight"

Synopsis

God's delight is salvation!

The Key Concepts of Sha'ashu'a

- Before the Tzimtzum, there was a higher dimensional Torah known as The Absolute.

- The Absolute consists of a mathematical language with coordinates.

- This is the infrastructure upon which the entirety of reality and consciousness is constructed.

- The Sod of Sha'ashu'a (refer to Sefirot; area which is equivalent to base of brain) is the consciousness of God.

- The Primordial Worlds that preceded Creation = Divine Ecstasy; compare foreplay vs orgasm.

- The "Secret of God" is the Primordial Torah = The Formula, YHVH.

- This is consciousness within consciousness.

- Sheer internal ecstasy emanated from within Ain Sof, manifesting as a dual rhythm oscillating outward, and then contracting.

- It looks like twinkling lights that created the Hebrew letters.

- It Delighted Itself; Orgasm; expanding and contracting pulses.

- All 22 letters of the Hebrew alphabet are contained within each other.

- Ohr Ain Sof means "Light of the never-ending" and is a fractal feedback loop that creates the toroid. This is perpetually self-creating, symbolized by the Silver Infinity Archetype.

- The "Fall" of the Absolute via Tzimtzum creates the Formula of YHVH, symbolized by 4 cubes within each other.

- YHVH creates 5 levels of Soul:

Chart of 5 Levels of Transmigrating Souls)

Alphanumeric Code In Tetragrammaton	World	Soul Level	SouloHoloarchy
Y-H-V-H / ה-ו-ה-י Crown Of Yud י	Adam Kadmon Primordial Man 5 Partzufim each with 10 Sefirot	Yechidah (Lit. "Singularity") Divine Essence 5th Level	Yechidah Chaya Neshama Ruach Nefesh
Yud י	Adam of Atzilut Emanation 5 Partzufim each with 10 Sefirot	Chaya (Lit. "Life") Living Essence 4th level	Yechidah Chaya Neshama Ruach Nefesh
Heh ה	Adam of Beriyah Creation 5 Partzufim each with 10 Sefirot	Neshama (Lit. "Breath") Breath 3rd level	Yechidah Chaya Neshama Ruach Nefesh
Vav ו	Adam of Yetzirah Formation 5 Partzufim each with 10 Sefirot	Ruach (Lit. "Wind") Spirit/Direction 2nd level	Yechidah Chaya Neshama Ruach Nefesh
Heh ה	Adam of Asiyah Completion/Action 5 Partzufim each with 10 Sefirot	Nefesh (Lit. "At rest") Animating Force 1st level	Yechidah Chaya Neshama Ruach Nefesh

courtesy of author Joel David Bakst © 2006

Talmud/Midrash Information

The Talmud and Midrash have information that is important in the context of history, spirituality/religion, and Self-growth.

- Many references are made to Yeshua Ha Notzri/Jesus the Nazarene.
- Christianity is the collective Soul of the Gentile Nations.
- Esau was the progenitor of Ancient Rome, incarnating into European and Russian nations.

- The Church censored most of this information during the Middle Ages.

- Most of this information is still being kept secret—or is it?

- Christianity is not what Christians believe it to be.

- A New Torah will be presented when the Messiah arrives.

- The New Torah will be the original Primordial Torah without physical rules.

- The relationship between Left Brain, Right Brain, and Pineal Gland is as follows:

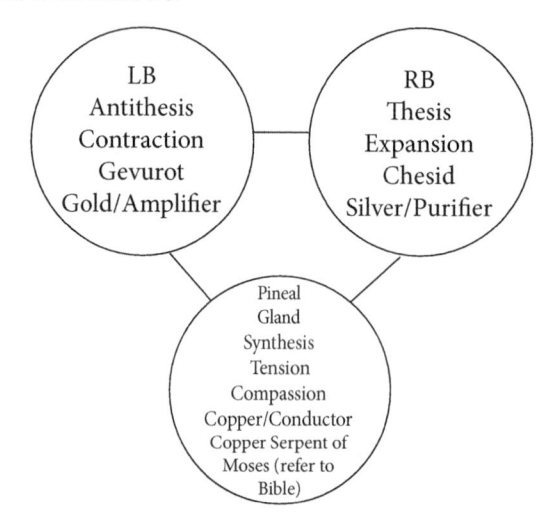

```
      LB                    RB
   Antithesis             Thesis
   Contraction          Expansion
    Gevurot              Chesid
 Gold/Amplifier       Silver/Purifier

           Pineal Gland
            Synthesis
             Tension
           Compassion
         Copper/Conductor
       Copper Serpent of Moses
          (refer to Bible)
```

- Judgment + Loving Kindness = Compassion.

- The Hebrew word for compassion is *Rachamim*.

- The root of Rachamim = *Rechem*, meaning womb, which is where mother and father meet to create.

- From the Torah perspective, there is no religion of Christianity or Islam.

- From the Torah perspective, Christianity and Islam are the Klipot/covering of Judaism.

Yod

וַעְשׂ = Esau

יַעְשׁוּעַ = Yeshua/Jesus

Esau and Yeshua have three common Hebrew letters.

When the Hebrew letter Yod is added to Esau, Esau becomes Yeshua/Salvation/Jesus.

Yod is the first letter for YHVH.

If Esau was the one not blessed by Isaac and then he was condemned to Edom and eventually Rome, could adding the Yod and creating Yeshua/Salvation be the manner in which God-Mind redeemed the descendants of Esau?

Gematria seems to explain this and justify why it was the Romans that had to conquer the Holy Land and deal with Jesus.

Every part of Creation is a fractal/fracture of existence. All pieces are part of the Whole. All space, time, history, and consciousness is compressed into a simple formula: YHVH.

YHVH means nothing when pronounced; it is not a word. YHVH is a formula or recipe. You cannot put 1 + 1 = 2 into a word. In Kabballah, YHVH is pronounced as "Havayah," which means "Existence."

Yod was used by the Greeks as *I*, pronounced "iota."

Yod was also used by the Latins as *J*, pronounced "jot."

Partzufim

Partzufim is another word for the Sefirot. Sefirot are explained as "The Light of Ain Sof," which is the mission and purpose of Creation.

Each Sefirot is like the rooms of the "home." They are the Faces of the Divine.

Tohu

The Tohu/chaos of the Absolute became a pattern/template for Creation via the Tzimtzum.

Translating Tohu as "chaos" is not exactly correct. A better translation is "organized energy in a pattern not yet understood."

Reincarnation

In ancient times, the doctrine of Reincarnation was always taught. When the Jews were removed to Rome after the destruction of the Second Temple, the Holy Roman Empire prohibited the preaching of such doctrines. Of course, it was removed from Christian religious texts as well.

Therefore, the teaching of Reincarnation went underground and was never taught in Hebrew schools. Reincarnation was only understood by the secret rabbis who studied Kaballah and Zohar, even to this day.

The Hebrew word for Reincarnation is *Gilgul*.

Gilgul means revolving or cycling through a lifetime. Gilgul is really about simultaneous manifestations rather than linear lifetimes.

Gal = Wave

Galgul = Wheel or iterations.

In Hebrew Gematria, Chesed/Loving Kindness = 72

Galgul = 72

The implication is that Reincarnation/Simultaneous Existence is a loving kindness to the Soul-personality to help with development.

The template of Adam Kadmon is based on Galgul; to keep iterations going until perfection returns to the original primordial version. This is the reason for the name "Adam."

In Hebrew, "Adam" has three root letters: Aleph, Daled, and Mem. In English, this would be: A, D, M.

These extrapolate to: Adam, David, and Moses. The M continues to Messiah from David, or Jmmanuel/Yehoshua/Yeshua.

All became martyrs in some fashion. All perished for "sins."

This became immortalized with the deaths of Rabbi Akiva (Rome) and the 10 Martyrs (Sefirot). It has been replayed throughout Jewish history via the Crusades, the Inquisition, The Holocaust and so forth.

Ten Martyrs

From Wikipedia, the free encyclopedia

The **Ten Martyrs** (Hebrew: עשרת הרוגי מלכות *Aseret Harugei Malchut*) were ten rabbis living during the era of the Mishnah who were martyred by the Roman Empire in the period after the destruction of the Second Temple. Their story is detailed in Midrash Eleh Ezkerah.

Although not killed at the same time (since two of the rabbis listed lived well before the other eight), a dramatic poem (known as *Eleh Ezkera*) tells their story as if they were killed together. This poem is recited on Yom Kippur, and a variation of it on Tisha BeAv.

Story as told in **Eleh Ezkerah**

In the story, the Roman emperor Hadrian decides to martyr ten rabbis as 'punishment' for the ten brothers listed in the Torah who sold their brother Joseph to Ancient Egypt. He justifies this by saying that the penalty for this was death. Though this crime took place almost 2000 years earlier, and Jewish law does not allow for the descendants of sinners to be punished, the Roman commander goes ahead with the executions because (he says) there are 'none like you' ten who are capable of rectifying this crime.

The martyrs

According to the poem, the first two to be executed were Rabban Shimon ben Gamliel and Rabbi Yishmael ben Elisha ha-Kohen Gadol. Rabban Shimon Ben Gamliel was beheaded, and while Rabbi Yishmael wept, the Roman ruler's daughter coveted Rabbi Yishmael for his physical beauty. When she was told that he would have to be executed as well, she asked that the skin of his head be flayed while he was alive, so she could stuff the skin and look at his face.

The most well known martyr is Rabbi Akiva, whose skin was raked with iron combs. Despite the pain consuming him, he was still able to proclaim God's providence in the world by reciting the Shema, drawing out the final *Echad* - "One".

Another sage martyred was Rabbi Haninah ben Teradion, who was wrapped in a Torah scroll and burned alive. Damp wool was packed into his chest to ensure he would not die quickly. When he was being burnt, he told his students that he could see the letters of the sacred torah "flying up" to heaven.

The others mentioned in the poem are Rabbi Hutzpit the Interpreter (so named, because he would interpret the words of the Rosh Yeshiva - the head of the Yeshiva - for the masses, who could not follow all his words); Rabbi Elazar ben Shamua; Rabbi Hanina ben Hakinai; Rabbi Yesheivav the Scribe; Rabbi Judah ben Dama; and Rabbi Judah ben Baba.

Listed Martyrs

Rabban Shimon ben Gamliel

Rabbi Yishmael ben Elisha ha-Kohen Gadol

Rabbi Akiva

Rabbi Haninah ben Teradion

Rabbi Hutzpit the Interpreter

Rabbi Elazar ben Shamua

Rabbi Hanina ben Hakinai

Rabbi Yesheivav the Scribe

Rabbi Judah ben Dama

Rabbi Judah ben Baba.

Historical evaluation

Contrary to the accounts given in the Talmud and in Midrash Rabbah, which clearly state that there were intervals between the executions of the ten teachers, the poem *Eleh Ezkerah* describes their martyrdom as occurring on the same day, probably in order to produce a greater effect upon the mind of the reader.

Popular imagination seized upon this episode in Jewish history, and embellished it with various legends relating the virtues of the martyrs and the fortitude shown by them during their execution. These legends became in the geonic period the subject of a special midrash—the Midrash 'Asarah Haruge Malkut, or Midrash Eleh Ezkerah. The deaths are described as being gruesome, including allegedly being wrapped in Torah scrolls and then being set aflame.

Use in ritual

The poem *Eleh Ezkerah* is best known as part of the Yom Kippur *mussaf* recital in the Ashkenazi ritual. This was made part of these services because of the impact losing so many pillars of Judaism would have to the masses. As such, it has become one of the 'highlights' of the day, marking a point when the congregation should reflect on their own lives and the sacrifices that were made for their sake.

A similar poem *Arzei haLevanon* is recited as one of the Kinot on Tisha B'Av.

Conservative Judaism's linkage

In contemporary times, the moral of this poem has taken on a new meaning with the deaths of millions of Jews during the Holocaust. Many Jews followed Rabbi Akiva's example reciting the Shema as they were being led to the gas chambers. A liturgical link was made explicit in the *Mahzor for Rosh Hashanah and Yom Kippur*, a 1972 project of the Rabbinical Assembly which is the primary rabbinical association for Conservative Judaism. In an elaborate reworking of the traditional text, the martyrology was interwoven with material from Hayyim Nahman Bialik, Hillel Bavli, and other sources, connecting the Roman persecutions to later persecutions such as those by the Russian Tsars and the Nazis. The section climaxes with a special version of Mourner's Kaddish which names sites of persecution and Jewish flourishing.

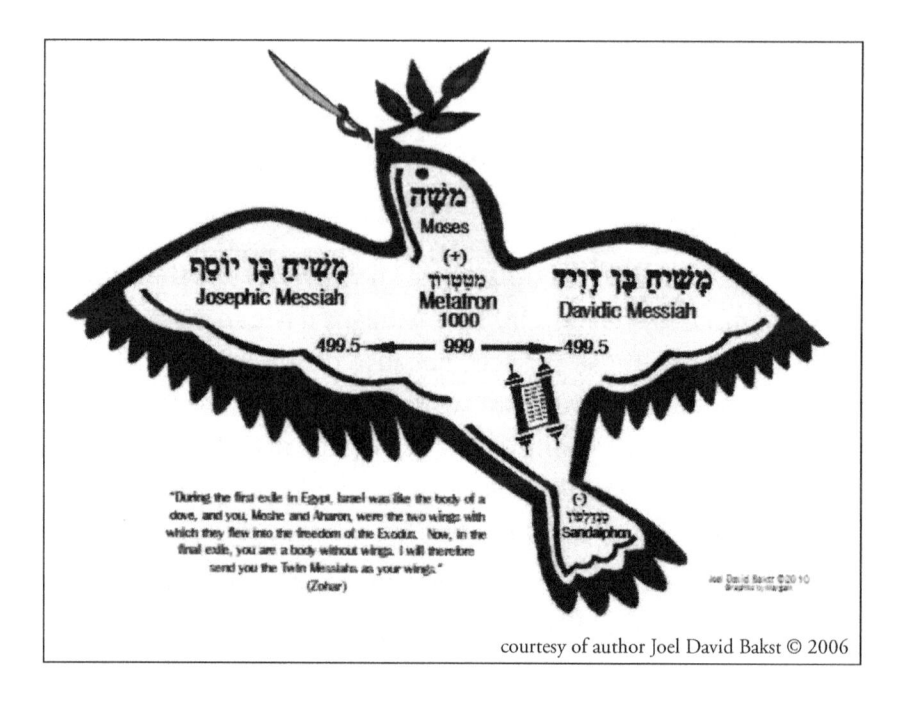

"During the first exile in Egypt, Israel was like the body of a dove, and you, Moshe and Aharon, were the two wings with which they flew into the freedom of the Exodus. Now, in the final exile, you are a body without wings. I will therefore send you the Twin Messiahs as your wings."
(Zohar)

courtesy of author Joel David Bakst © 2006

The Bahir

The Bahir is the oldest and most secret book in the Kaballah. *Bahir* means "Brilliance." This book, according to Kabalistic tradition, is supposed to be a crown for your head.

The Bahir was written by Rabbi Nehuniah ben HaKana in the First Century. But, his name is never mentioned after the first paragraph. The real name may be Rabbi Amorai. That name means, "speakers." He may have been a member of the Essenes.

The book goes on to state that Rabbi Shimon emerged from a cave where the Books of the Zohar were revealed to him. From these books, and from The Bahir, it is said that Rabba The Great One and Rav Zeira in Babylon, during the Fourth Century, performed miraculous cures and created living creatures! Amazing! Could the Golem of Prague be a result of such works as well?

Hekhalot is a section of The Bahir that teaches how to project into other universes!

The Bahir says that the "Workings of the Chariot"/*Ma'aseh Merkava*, cannot be taught to a single individual, unless he is wise enough. In this case, the word "chariot" refers to the energy field of the human body.

The Bahir contains 5 parts:
1. First verses of creation.
2. The alphabet.
3. The 7 Voices and Sefirot.
4. The 10 Sefirot.
5. The Mysteries of the Soul.

Some of the salient points of this book are:

- *Saper* is the root word of Sefirot.
- *Saper* means "God's Power & Glory."
- Reincarnation is Divine Justice.
- There are masculine and feminine souls.
- The Kaballah should only be taught via hints and allusions; reading it literally will lead to certain misunderstandings.
- All Kaballah texts must be seen as a whole, then use the parts to understand other parts.
- Angels are Directors and Functionaries.
- The Name of God has 72 combinations.
- There is no empty space.
- His Will decided to create all universes.
- He constricted Himself (Tzimtzum) from perfectly round and entered a single thread of Infinite Light. This is analogous to a sperm entering an egg.

- From this thread, all Creation took place.
- Tzimtzum is not to be taken literally since it is impossible to apply any special concept to God.
- There is no place empty of Him.
- The Sefirot are the bridge between God and Universes.
- *Tohu* = chaos/confounded.
- *Bohu* = Desolation/not formed.
- Tohu and Bohu are both ingredients of Creation.
- Bohu is actually the two words of *Bo* and *Hu*, which together mean, "It is in it."
- Keter/Crown means "above the mind's ability to understand."
- Creation is "something" from "nothing."
- *Berakhah* means Blessing.
- *Berekh* is the root word of Berakhah. Berekh means "knee," which is why you bend the knee when you pray.
- Levels and correlations of Existence:

'''	Adam Kadmon	Primordial	Mind	Uniqueness	Crown
Y	Atzilut	Nearness	Eyes	Vitality	Wisdom
H	Beriyah	Creation	Ears	Breath	Understanding
V	Yetzirah	Formation	Nose	Wind	Next 6 Sefirot
H	Asiyah	Making	Mouth	Soul	Kingship

- Peace = Reconciliation between ultimate opposites. accomplished through creation of evil.
- Silver = Love. Should be given out.
- Gold = Strength. Should be held.
- Covenant = Sefirot of Yesod, foundation; male sex organ.

154 • Revelations of Time & Space, History and God

- Circumcision is the removal of klipot to transmit souls that are "knowing."
- Shalom = Peace/Shalem = Perfect and complete.

Aleph is made of 2 Yods and 1 Vov.

אׇ

- Mikvah is a Ritual bath that contains 40 measures of natural source water; it replicates the womb and the person emerges reborn; the original Baptism.
- There are 32 paths to God comprised of the 22 letters of Hebrew alphabet + 10 vowels.
- The 32 paths to God are represented by the connections between Sefirot.

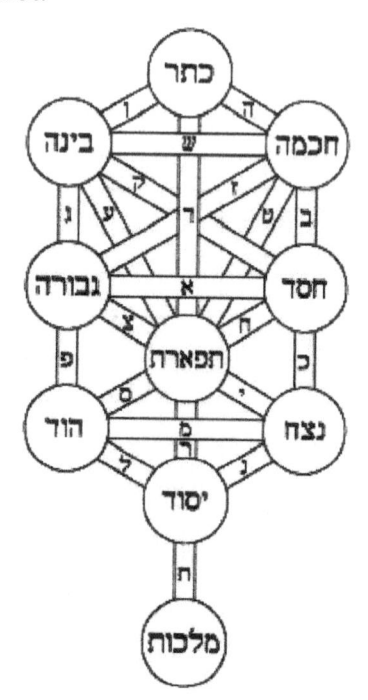

- The Torah says that Adam was created in "an" image of God,
- Male + Female/Androgynous
- Eve was created from a *tzela,* meaning "side"—not a rib. Therefore, one of the "sides" of Androgynous Adam was female.
- Most references in The Bahir are sexual.
- The Bahir describes each Hebrew letter and how they can be converted into each other.
- You can spend more than a lifetime just studying a few chapters of the Book of the Bahir.

The Thomas Code/Gospel of Thomas

This little known document by the twin of Jmmanuel was first discovered in small fragments in 1897 with a few more discovered in 1903. Then, in 1945, in Nag Hammadi, Egypt, entire scrolls were found in buried jars.

These scrolls were written in Syriac, a dialect of Aramaic. The Gospel has been pieced together over decades. Interestingly, the scrolls document events as they happened by personal witnesses as opposed to Canonized Gospels that were written decades and even centuries after-the-fact.

There are 108 sayings in this Gospel. Whoever created this Gospel understood deep symbolism, advanced mathematics, and must have known that at the correct time in the future, people would understand.

Why 108? This number is very significant, as per Wikipedia:

In mathematics 108 is:

an abundant number.

a semiperfect number.

a tetranacci number.

the hyperfactorial of 3 since it is of the form.

divisible by the value of its φ function, which is 36.

divisible by the total number of its divisors (12), hence it is a refactorable number.

the angle in degrees of the interior angles of a regular pentagon in Euclidean space.

palindromic in bases 11 (99_{11}), 17 (66_{17}), 26 (44_{26}), 35 (33_{35}) and 53 (22_{53})

a Harshad number in bases 2, 3, 4, 6, 7, 9, 10, 11, 12, 13 and 16

a self number.

nine dozen

There are 108 free polyominoes of order 7.

The equation results in the golden ratio.

Religion and the arts

The number 108 is considered sacred by the Dharmic Religions, such as Hinduism, Buddhism, and Jainism.

Hinduism

In Hindu tradition, the Mukhya Shivaganas (attendants of Shiva) are 108 in number and hence Shaiva religions, particularly Lingayats, use malas of 108 beads for prayer and meditation.

Similarly, in Gaudiya Vaishnavism, Lord Krishna in Brindavan had 108 followers known as gopis. Recital of their names, often accompanied by the counting of a 108-beaded mala, is often done during religious ceremonies. The Sri Vaishnavite Tradition has 108 Divya Desams (temples of Vishnu) that are revered by the 12 Alvars in the *Divya Prabandha*, a collection of 4,000 Tamil verses.

Jainism

In Jainism, the total number of ways of Karma influx (Aasrav). 4 Kashays (anger, pride, conceit, greed) x 3 karanas (mind, speech, bodily action) x 3 stages of planning (planning, procurement, commencement) x 3 ways of execution (own action, getting it done, supporting or approval of action).

Buddhism

In Buddhism, according to Bhante Gunaratana this number is reached by multiplying the senses smell, touch, taste, hearing, sight, and consciousness by whether they are painful, pleasant or neutral, and then again by whether these are internally generated or externally occurring, and yet again by past, present and future, finally we get 108 feelings. 6 × 3 × 2 × 3 = 108.

Tibetan Buddhist malas or rosaries are usually 108 beads; sometimes 111 including the guru bead(s), reflecting the words of the Buddha called in Tibetan the Kangyur (Wylie: Bka'-'gyur) in 108 volumes. Zen priests wear juzu (a ring of prayer beads) around their wrists, which consists of 108 beads.

Japa mala, or *japa beads*, made from tulasi wood, consisting of 108 beads plus the head bead.

The Lankavatara Sutra has a section where the Bodhisattva Mahamati asks Buddha 108 questions and another section where Buddha lists 108 statements of negation in the form of "A statement concerning X is not a statement concerning X." In a footnote, D.T. Suzuki explains that the Sanskrit word translated as "statement" is *pada* which can also mean "foot-step" or "a position." This confusion over the word "pada" explains why some have mistakenly held that the reference to 108 statements in the Lankavatara refer to the 108 steps that many temples have.

In Japan, at the end of the year, a bell is chimed 108 times in Buddhist temples to finish the old year and welcome the new one. Each ring represents one of 108 earthly temptations (Bonnō) a person must overcome to achieve nirvana.

Other references

In the neo-Gnostic teachings of Samael Aun Weor, an individual has 108 chances (lifetimes) to eliminate his egos and transcend the material world before "devolving" and having the egos forcefully removed in the infradimensions.

Martial arts

Many East Asian martial arts trace their roots back to Buddhism, specifically, to the Buddhist Shaolin Temple. Because of their ties to Buddhism, 108 has become an important symbolic number in a number of martial arts styles.

According to Marma Adi and Ayurveda, there are 108 pressure points in the body, where consciousness and flesh intersect to give life to the living being.

The Chinese school of martial arts agrees with the South Indian school of martial arts on the principle of 108 pressure points.

108 number figures prominently in the symbolism associated with karate, particularly the Gōjū-ryū discipline. The ultimate Gōjū-ryū kata, *Suparinpei*, literally translates to 108. *Suparinpei* is the Chinese pronunciation of the number 108, while *gojūshi* of Gojūshiho is the Japanese pronunciation of the number 54. The other Gōjū-ryū kata, *Sanseru* (meaning "36") and *Seipai* ("18") are factors of the number 108.

The 108 moves of the Yang Taijiquan long form and 108 moves in the Wing Chun wooden dummy form, taught by Ip Man, are noted in this regard.

The Eagle Claw Kung Fu style has a form known as the 108 Locking Hand Techniques. This form is considered the essence of the style, consisting of an encyclopedia of Chin Na techniques, and is said to be passed down from the founder General Yue Fei.

Paek Pal Ki Hyung, the 7th form taught in the art of Kuk Sool Won, translates literally to "108 technique" form. It is also frequently referred to as the "eliminate 108 torments" form. Each motion corresponds with one of the 108 Buddhist torments or defilements.

In literature

In Homer's *Odyssey*, the number of suitors coveting Penelope, wife of Odysseus.

There are 108 outlaws in the Chinese classic *Water Margin/Outlaws of the Marsh* by Shi Nai'an.

There are 108 love sonnets in *Astrophil and Stella*, the first English sonnet sequence by Sir Philip Sidney.

In science

108 is the atomic number of hassium.

108 degrees Fahrenheit is the internal temperature at which the human body's vital organs begin to fail from overheating.

The distance of Earth from the Sun is about 108 times the diameter of the Sun (actually closer to 107.51, as per definition of the AU). Actual ratio varies between 105.7 (Perihelion) and 109.3 (Aphelion).

"The Gospel of Thomas" is divided into 6 sets of 18 sayings. Number 18 in Hebrew Gematria is from the word *Chai*, which means "Life."

Because Existence is fractal, the Number 18 can be "fractalized," or factored into prime numbers.

$$108 = 2^2 \times 3^3$$

In other words,

$$108 = 2 \times 2 \times 3 \times 3 \times 3$$

In "The Gospel of Thomas," the sayings have a pattern of:

3 x 2 x 3 x 2 x 3

This numerical pattern demonstrates the Twinning of Christ/Thomas as well as the Trinity of:

Father-Son-Holy Spirit.

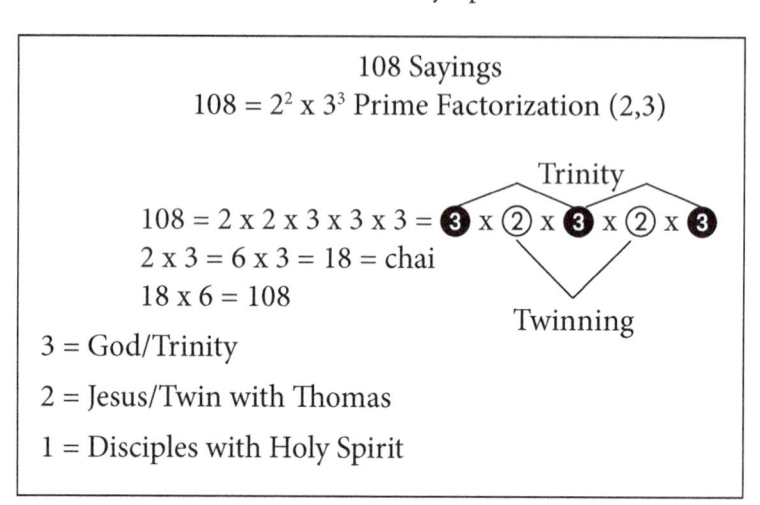

---

108 Sayings
$108 = 2^2 \times 3^3$ Prime Factorization (2,3)

$108 = 2 \times 2 \times 3 \times 3 \times 3 =$ ③ x ② x ③ x ② x ③   (Trinity / Twinning)

$2 \times 3 = 6 \times 3 = 18 =$ chai

$18 \times 6 = 108$

3 = God/Trinity

2 = Jesus/Twin with Thomas

1 = Disciples with Holy Spirit

The Star of David has 6 points.

18 x 6 = 108

In the Gospels of Matthew and Luke, which were written much later, it is apparent that "The Gospel of Thomas" was used as a source as well as "The Gospel of Q." "The Gospel of Q" is included in *The Template of God-Mind.*

"The Gospel of Thomas" is original. All sayings begin with, "Jesus said…" These are direct quotes.

There are many coded messages in the sayings. For example, "Jesus said, I shall choose 1 out of 1000."

1000 is the Metatron Messianic number code.

$1000 = 2^3 \times 5^3$. Or, $(2 \times 5)^3$.

All numbers mentioned in the Bible are based on the Thomas Code, which is to factor a number into its Prime Numbers.

For example, use the story of Jesus feeding 5000 with 2 loaves of bread and 5 fish.

Thomas Code Pattern: $3 \times 2 \times 3 \times 2 \times 3 = 108$

5000 to be fed: $5 \times 2 \times 5 \times 2 \times 5 \times 2 \times 5 = 5000$

Zohar and Kaballah use the Thomas Code as appropriate. Read the complete "Gospel of Thomas" for further information and understanding.

Gospel of Thomas
(Translated by Thomas O. Lambdin)

These are the secret sayings which the living Jesus spoke and which Didymos Judas Thomas wrote down. (1) And he said, "Whoever finds the interpretation of these sayings will not experience death." (2) Jesus said, "Let him who seeks continue seeking until he finds. When he finds, he will become troubled. When he becomes troubled, he will be astonished, and he will rule over the All." (3) Jesus said, "If those who lead you say to you, 'See, the kingdom is in the sky,' then the birds of the sky will precede you. If they say to you, 'It is in the sea,' then the fish will precede you. Rather, the kingdom is inside of you, and it is outside of you. When you come to know yourselves, then you will become known, and you will realize that it is you who are the sons of the living father. But if you will not know yourselves, you dwell in poverty and it is you who are that poverty." (4) Jesus said, "The man old in days will not hesitate to ask a small child seven days old about the place of life, and he will live. For many who are first will become last, and they will become one and the same." (5) Jesus said, "Recognize what is in your sight, and that which is hidden from you will become plain to you. For there is nothing hidden which will not become manifest." (6) His disciples questioned him and said to him, "Do you want us to fast? How shall we pray? Shall we give alms? What diet shall we observe?" Jesus said, "Do not tell lies, and do not do what you hate, for all things are plain in the sight of heaven. For nothing hidden will not become manifest, and nothing covered will remain without being uncovered." (7) Jesus said, "Blessed is the lion which becomes man when consumed by man; and cursed is the man whom the lion consumes, and the lion becomes man." (8) And he said, "The man is like a wise fisherman who cast his net into the sea and drew it up from the sea full of small fish. Among them the wise fisherman found a fine large fish. He threw all the small fish back into the sea and chose the large fish without difficulty. Whoever has ears to hear, let him hear." 1 (9) Jesus said, "Now the sower went out, took a handful (of seeds), and scattered them. Some fell on the road; the birds came and gathered them up. Others fell on the rock, did not take root in the soil, and did not produce ears. And others fell on thorns; they choked the seed(s) and worms ate them. And others fell on the good soil and it produced good fruit: it bore sixty per measure and a hundred and twenty per measure." (10) Jesus said, "I have cast fire upon the world, and see, I am guarding it until it blazes." (11) Jesus said, "This heaven will pass away, and the one above it will pass away. The dead are not alive, and the living will not die. In the days when you consumed what is dead, you made it what is alive. When you come to dwell in the light, what will you do? On the day when you were one you became two. But when you become two, what will you do?" (12) The disciples said to Jesus, "We know that you will depart from us. Who is to be our leader?" Jesus said to them, "Wherever you are, you are to go to James the righteous, for whose sake heaven and earth came into being." (13) Jesus said to his disciples, "Compare me to someone and tell me whom I am like." Simon Peter said to him, "You are like a righteous angel." Matthew said to him, "You are like a wise philosopher." Thomas said to him, "Master, my mouth is wholly incapable of saying whom you are like." Jesus said, "I am not your master. Because you have drunk, you have become intoxicated from the bubbling spring which I have measured out." And he took him and withdrew and told him three things. When Thomas returned to his companions, they asked him, "What did Jesus say to you?" Thomas said to them, "If I tell you one of the things which he told me, you will pick up stones and throw them at me; a fire will come out of the stones and burn you up." (14) Jesus said to them, "If you fast, you will give rise to sin for yourselves; and if you pray, you will be condemned; and if you give alms, you will do harm to your spirits. When you go into any land and walk about in the districts, if they receive you, eat what they will set before you, and heal the sick among them. For what goes into your mouth will not defile you, but that which issues from your mouth - it is that which will defile you." (15) Jesus said, "When you see one who was not born of woman, prostrate yourselves on your faces and worship him. That one is your father." (16) Jesus said, "Men think, perhaps, that it is peace which I have come to cast upon the world. They do not know that it is dissension which I have come to cast upon the earth:

fire, sword, and war. For there will be five in a house: three will be against two, and two against three, the father against the son, and the son against the father. And they will stand solitary." 2 (17) Jesus said, "I shall give you what no eye has seen and what no ear has heard and what no hand has touched and what has never occurred to the human mind." (18) The disciples said to Jesus, "Tell us how our end will be." Jesus said, "Have you discovered, then, the beginning, that you look for the end? For where the beginning is, there will the end be. Blessed is he who will take his place in the beginning; he will know the end and will not experience death." (19) Jesus said, "Blessed is he who came into being before he came into being. If you become my disciples and listen to my words, these stones will minister to you. For there are five trees for you in Paradise which remain undisturbed summer and winter and whose leaves do not fall. Whoever becomes acquainted with them will not experience death." (20) The disciples said to Jesus, "Tell us what the kingdom of heaven is like." He said to them, "It is like a mustard seed. It is the smallest of all seeds. But when it falls on tilled soil, it produces a great plant and becomes a shelter for birds of the sky." (21) Mary said to Jesus, "Whom are your disciples like?" He said, "They are like children who have settled in a field which is not theirs. When the owners of the field come, they will say, 'Let us have back our field.' They (will) undress in their presence in order to let them have back their field and to give it back to them. Therefore I say, if the owner of a house knows that the thief is coming, he will begin his vigil before he comes and will not let him dig through into his house of his domain to carry away his goods. You, then, be on your guard against the world. Arm yourselves with great strength lest the robbers find a way to come to you, for the difficulty which you expect will (surely) materialize. Let there be among you a man of understanding. When the grain ripened, he came quickly with his sickle in his hand and reaped it. Whoever has ears to hear, let him hear." (22) Jesus saw infants being suckled. He said to his disciples, "These infants being suckled are like those who enter the kingdom." They said to him, "Shall we then, as children, enter the kingdom?" Jesus said to them, "When you make the two one, and when you make the inside like the outside and the outside like the inside, and the above like the below, and when you make the male and the female one and the same, so that the male not be male nor the female; and when you fashion eyes in the place of an eye, and a hand in place of a hand, and a foot in place of a foot, and a likeness in place of a likeness; then will you enter the kingdom." (23) Jesus said, "I shall choose you, one out of a thousand, and two out of ten thousand, and they shall stand as a single one." (24) His disciples said to him, "Show us the place where you are, since it is necessary for us to seek it." 3 He said to them, "Whoever has ears, let him hear. There is light within a man of light, and he lights up the whole world. If he does not shine, he is darkness." (25) Jesus said, "Love your brother like your soul, guard him like the pupil of your eye." (26) Jesus said, "You see the mote in your brother's eye, but you do not see the beam in your own eye. When you cast the beam out of your own eye, then you will see clearly to cast the mote from your brother's eye." (27) "If you do not fast as regards the world, you will not find the kingdom. If you do not observe the Sabbath as a Sabbath, you will not see the father." (28) Jesus said, "I took my place in the midst of the world, and I appeared to them in flesh. I found all of them intoxicated; I found none of them thirsty. And my soul became afflicted for the sons of men, because they are blind in their hearts and do not have sight; for empty they came into the world, and empty too they seek to leave the world. But for the moment they are intoxicated. When they shake off their wine, then they will repent." (29) Jesus said, "If the flesh came into being because of spirit, it is a wonder. But if spirit came into being because of the body, it is a wonder of wonders. Indeed, I am amazed at how this great wealth has made its home in this poverty." (30) Jesus said, "Where there are three gods, they are gods. Where there are two or one, I am with him." (31) Jesus said, "No prophet is accepted in his own village; no physician heals those who know him." (32) Jesus said, "A city being built on a high mountain and fortified cannot fall, nor can it be hidden." (33) Jesus said, "Preach from your housetops that which you will hear in your ear. For no one lights a lamp and puts it under a bushel, nor does he put it in a hidden place, but rather he sets it on a lamp stand so that everyone who enters and leaves will see its light." (34) Jesus said, "If a blind man leads a blind man, they will both fall into a pit." (35) Jesus said, "It is not possible for anyone to enter the house of a strong man and take it by force unless he binds his hands; then he will (be able to) ransack his house." (36) Jesus said, "Do not be concerned from morning until evening and from evening until morning about what you will wear." (37) His disciples said, "When will you become revealed to us and when shall we see you?" 4 Jesus said, "When you disrobe without being ashamed and take up your garments and place them under your feet like little children and tread on them, then will you see the son of the living one, and you will not be afraid" (38) Jesus said, "Many times have you desired to hear these words which I am saying to you, and you have no one else to hear them from. There will be days when you will look for me and will not find me." (39) Jesus said, "The pharisees and the scribes have taken the keys of knowledge (gnosis) and hidden them. They themselves have not entered, nor have they allowed to enter those who wish to. You, however, be as wise as serpents and as innocent as doves." (40) Jesus said, "A grapevine has been planted outside of the father, but being unsound, it will be pulled up by its roots and destroyed." (41) Jesus said, "Whoever has something in his hand will receive more, and whoever has nothing will be deprived of even the little he has." (42) Jesus said, "Become passers-by." (43) His disciples said to him, "Who are you, that you should say these things to us?" "You do not realize who I am from what I say to you, but you have become like the Jews, for they (either) love the tree and hate its fruit (or) love the fruit and hate the tree." (44) Jesus said, "Whoever blasphemes against the father will be forgiven, and whoever blasphemes against the son will be forgiven, but whoever blasphemes against the holy spirit will not be forgiven either on earth or in heaven." (45) Jesus said, "Grapes are not harvested from thorns, nor are figs gathered from thistles, for they do not produce fruit. A good man brings forth good from his storehouse; an evil man brings forth evil things from his evil storehouse, which is in his heart, and says evil things. For out of the abundance of the heart he brings forth evil things." (46) Jesus said, "Among those born of women, from Adam until John the Baptist, there is no one so superior to John the Baptist that his eyes should not be lowered (before him). Yet I have said, whichever one of you comes to be a child will be acquainted with the kingdom and will become superior to John." (47) Jesus said, "It is impossible for a man to mount two horses or to stretch two bows. And it is impossible for a servant to serve two masters;

otherwise, he will honor the one and treat the other contemptuously. No man drinks old wine and immediately desires to drink new wine. And new wine is not put into old wineskins, lest they burst; nor is old wine put into a new wineskin, lest it spoil it. An old patch is not sewn onto a new garment, because a tear would result." 5 (48) Jesus said, "If two make peace with each other in this one house, they will say to the mountain, 'Move Away,' and it will move away." (49) Jesus said, "Blessed are the solitary and elect, for you will find the kingdom. For you are from it, and to it you will return." (50) Jesus said, "If they say to you, 'Where did you come from?', say to them, 'We came from the light, the place where the light came into being on its own accord and established itself and became manifest through their image.' If they say to you, 'Is it you?', say, 'We are its children, we are the elect of the living father.' If they ask you, 'What is the sign of your father in you?', say to them, 'It is movement and repose.'" (51) His disciples said to him, "When will the repose of the dead come about, and when will the new world come?" He said to them, "What you look forward to has already come, but you do not recognize it." (52) His disciples said to him, "Twenty-four prophets spoke in Israel, and all of them spoke in you." He said to them, "You have omitted the one living in your presence and have spoken (only) of the dead." (53) His disciples said to him, "Is circumcision beneficial or not?" He said to them, "If it were beneficial, their father would beget them already circumcised from their mother. Rather, the true circumcision in spirit has become completely profitable." (54) Jesus said, "Blessed are the poor, for yours is the kingdom of heaven." (55) Jesus said, "Whoever does not hate his father and his mother cannot become a disciple to me. And whoever does not hate his brothers and sisters and take up his cross in my way will not be worthy of me." (56) Jesus said, "Whoever has come to understand the world has found (only) a corpse, and whoever has found a corpse is superior to the world." (57) Jesus said, "The kingdom of the father is like a man who had good seed. His enemy came by night and sowed weeds among the good seed. The man did not allow them to pull up the weeds; he said to them, 'I am afraid that you will go intending to pull up the weeds and pull up the wheat along with them.' For on the day of the harvest the weeds will be plainly visible, and they will be pulled up and burned." (58) Jesus said, "Blessed is the man who has suffered and found life." 6 (59) Jesus said, "Take heed of the living one while you are alive, lest you die and seek to see him and be unable to do so." (60) a Samaritan carrying a lamb on his way to Judea. He said to his disciples, "That man is round about the lamb." They said to him, "So that he may kill it and eat it." He said to them, "While it is alive, he will not eat it, but only when he has killed it and it has become a corpse." They said to him, "He cannot do so otherwise." He said to them, "You too, look for a place for yourself within repose, lest you become a corpse and be eaten." (61) Jesus said, "Two will rest on a bed: the one will die, and the other will live." Salome said, "Who are you, man, that you ... have come up on my couch and eaten from my table?" Jesus said to her, "I am he who exists from the undivided. I was given some of the things of my father." "I am your disciple." "Therefore I say, if he is destroyed, he will be filled with light, but if he is divided, he will be filled with darkness." (62) Jesus said, "It is to those who are worthy of my mysteries that I tell my mysteries. Do not let your left (hand) know what your right (hand) is doing." (63) Jesus said, "There was a rich man who had much money. He said, 'I shall put my money to use so that I may sow, reap, plant, and fill my storehouse with produce, with the result that I shall lack nothing.' Such were his intentions, but that same night he died. Let him who has ears hear." (64) Jesus said, "A man had received visitors. And when he had prepared the dinner, he sent his servant to invite the guests. He went to the first one and said to him, 'My master invites you.' He said, 'I have claims against some merchants. They are coming to me this evening. I must go and give them my orders. I ask to be excused from the dinner.' He went to another and said to him, 'My master has invited you.' He said to him, 'I have just bought a house and am required for the day. I shall not have any spare time.' He went to another and said to him, 'My master invites you.' He said to him, 'My friend is going to get married, and I am to prepare the banquet. I shall not be able to come. I ask to be excused from the dinner.' He went to another and said to him, 'My master invites you.' He said to him, 'I have just bought a farm, and I am on my way to collect the rent. I shall not be able to come. I ask to be excused.' The servant returned and said to his master, 'Those whom you invited to the dinner have asked to be excused.' The master said to his servant, 'Go outside to the streets and bring back those whom you happen to meet, so that they may dine.' Businessmen and merchants will not enter the places of my father." 7 (65) He said, "There was a good man who owned a vineyard. He leased it to tenant farmers so that they might work it and he might collect the produce from them. He sent his servant so that the tenants might give him the produce of the vineyard. They seized his servant and beat him, all but killing him. The servant went back and told his master. The master said, 'Perhaps he did not recognize them.' He sent another servant. The tenants beat this one as well.

Then the owner sent his son and said, 'Perhaps they will show respect to my son.' Because the tenants knew that it was he who was the heir to the vineyard, they seized him and killed him. Let him who has ears hear." (66) Jesus said, "Show me the stone which the builders have rejected. That one is the cornerstone." (67) Jesus said, "If one who knows the all still feels a personal deficiency, he is completely deficient." (68) Jesus said, "Blessed are you when you are hated and persecuted. Wherever you have been persecuted they will find no place." (69) Jesus said, "Blessed are they who have been persecuted within themselves. It is they who have truly come to know the father. Blessed are the hungry, for the belly of him who desires will be filled." (70) Jesus said, "That which you have will save you if you bring it forth from yourselves. That which you do not have within you will kill you if you do not have it within you." (71) Jesus said, "I shall destroy this house, and no one will be able to build it [...]." (72) A man said to him, "Tell my brothers to divide my father's possessions with me." He said to him, "O man, who has made me a divider?" He turned to his disciples and said to them, "I am not a divider, am I?" (73) Jesus said, "The harvest is great but the laborers are few. Beseech the Lord, therefore, to send out laborers to the harvest." (74) He said, "O Lord, there are many around the drinking trough, but there is nothing in the cistern." (75) Jesus said, "Many are standing at the door, but it is the solitary who will enter the bridal chamber." (76) Jesus said, "The kingdom of the father is like a merchant who had a consignment of merchandise and who discovered a pearl. That merchant was shrewd. He sold the merchandise and bought the pearl alone for himself. You too, seek his unfailing and enduring treasure where no moth comes near to devour and no worm destroys." 8 (77) Jesus said, "It is I who am the light which is above them all. It is I who am the all. From me did the all come forth, and unto me did the all extend. Split a piece of wood, and I am there. Lift up the stone, and you will find me there." (78) Jesus said, "Why have you come out into the desert? To see a reed shaken by the wind? And to see a man clothed in fine garments like your kings and your great men? Upon them are the fine garments, and they are unable to discern the truth." (79) A woman from the crowd said to him, "Blessed are the womb which bore you and the breasts which nourished you." He said to her, "Blessed are those who have heard the word of the father and have truly kept it. For there will be days when you will say, 'Blessed are the womb which has not conceived and the breasts which have not given milk.'" (80) Jesus said, "He who has recognized the world has found the body, but he who has found the body is superior to the world." (81) Jesus said, "Let him who has grown rich be king, and let him who possesses power renounce it." (82) Jesus said, "He who is near me is near the fire, and he who is far from me is far from the kingdom." (83) Jesus said, "The images are manifest to man, but the light in them remains concealed in the image of the light of the father. He will become manifest, but his image will remain concealed by his light." (84) Jesus said, "When you see your likeness, you rejoice. But when you see your images which came into being before you, and which neither die not become manifest, how much you will have to bear!" (85) Jesus said, "Adam came into being from a great power and a great wealth, but he did not become worthy of you. For had he been worthy, he would not have experienced death." (86) Jesus said, "The foxes have their holes and the birds have their nests, but the son of man has no place to lay his head and rest." (87) Jesus said, "Wretched is the body that is dependant upon a body, and wretched is the soul that is dependent on these two." (88) Jesus said, "The angels and the prophets will come to you and give to you those things you (already) have. And you too, give them those things which you have, and say to yourselves, 'When will they come and take what is theirs?'" 9 (89) Jesus said, "Why do you wash the outside of the cup? Do you not realize that he who made the inside is the same one who made the outside?" (90) Jesus said, "Come unto me, for my yoke is easy and my lordship is mild, and you will find repose for yourselves." (91) They said to him, "Tell us who you are so that we may believe in you." He said to them, "You read the face of the sky and of the earth, but you have not recognized the one who is before you, and you do not know how to read this moment." (92) Jesus said, "Seek and you will find. Yet, what you asked me about in former times and which I did not tell you then, now I do desire to tell, but you do not inquire after it." (93) "Do not give what is holy to dogs, lest they throw them on the dungheap. Do not throw the pearls to swine, lest they [...] it [...]." (94) Jesus said, "He who seeks will find, and he who knocks will be let in." (95) Jesus said, "If you have money, do not lend it at interest, but give it to one from whom you will not get it back." (96) Jesus said, "The kingdom of the father is like a certain woman. She took a little leaven, concealed it in some dough, and made it into large loaves. Let him who has ears hear." (97) Jesus said, "The kingdom of the father is like a certain woman who was carrying a jar full of meal. While she was walking on the road, still some distance from home, the handle of the jar broke and the meal emptied out behind her on the road. She did not realize it; she had noticed no accident. When she reached her house, she set the jar down and found it empty." (98) Jesus said, "The kingdom of the father is like a certain man who wanted to kill a powerful man. In his own house he drew his sword and stuck it into the wall in order to find out whether his hand could carry through. Then he slew the powerful man." (99) The disciples said to him, "Your brothers and your mother are standing outside." He said to them, "Those here who do the will of my father are my brothers and my mother. It is they who will enter the kingdom of my father." (100) They showed Jesus a gold coin and said to him, "Caesar's men demand taxes from us." He said to them, "Give Caesar what belongs to Caesar, give God what belongs to God, and give me what is mine." 10 (101) "Whoever does not hate his father and his mother as I do cannot become a disciple to me. And whoever does not love his father and his mother as I do cannot become a disciple to me. For my mother [...], but my true mother gave me life." (102) Jesus said, "Woe to the pharisees, for they are like a dog sleeping in the manger of oxen, for neither does he eat nor does he let the oxen eat." (103) Jesus said, "Fortunate is the man who knows where the brigands will enter, so that he may get up, muster his domain, and arm himself before they invade." (104) They said to Jesus, "Come, let us pray today and let us fast." Jesus said, "What is the sin that I have committed, or wherein have I been defeated? But when the bridegroom leaves the bridal chamber, then let them fast and pray." (105) Jesus said, "He who knows the father and the mother will be called the son of a harlot." (106) Jesus said, "When you make the two one, you will become the sons of man, and when you say, 'Mountain, move away,' it will move away." (107) Jesus said, "The kingdom is like a shepherd who had a hundred sheep. One of them, the largest, went astray. He left the ninety-nine sheep and looked for that one until he found it. When he had gone to such trouble, he said to the sheep, 'I care for you more than the ninety-nine.'" (108) Jesus said, "He who will drink from my mouth will become like me. I myself shall become he, and the things that are hidden will be revealed to him."

There are 12 main themes in "The Gospel of Thomas"

$$12 = 2 \times 3 \times 2$$

There are 12 Tribes + 12 Zodiac Signs + 12 Months = 36

$$36 = 2 \times 18$$

or

$$3 \times 2 \times 3 = 18$$

Therefore: $3 \times 2 \times 3 \times 2 \times 3 = 108$.

12 Main Themes of "The Gospel of Thomas"

Theme	*Meaning*
Seek and find.	Answers for all who ask
The first shall be last.	There is no time or space
Being troubled and amazed.	Tribulation results in awareness
Evil mustard seed.	The tiniest seed becomes a strong tree
None other from whom to hear them.	Messiah
Accepted and rejected.	Discernment
Moving the mountain.	All obstacles can be surpassed
The question not answered.	Must be ready for truth
Answers not asked for.	You need what you do not expect
No place to rest.	Humankind should have a knowing
Shepherd to lost sheep.	God and Humankind
Mary Magdalene is the final answer.	Shekhinah

These 12 Themes and Meanings are points of study for a lifetime. The answers can be found within the Torah, Kaballah, and Zohar.

St. Thomas, the twin of Jmmanuel/Yehoshua/Yeshua, created original Christianity in India based on Judaism and Torah circa 60 AD when he arrived and found remnants of the Lost Tribes.

When the Portuguese Catholics arrived in Goa in the 1500s, they discovered these Jewish-Christians. The Jewish-Christians were ordered to convert to Catholicism and pledge allegiance to the Vatican, or be executed. Many chose death.

Others were able to flee to what is now Iraq, which was a Christian country. In Baghdad, the descendants of Thomas and his followers established the Chaldean Church of the East. Today, in the 21st Century, Chaldean Church of the East is based in Brazil for safety reasons.

Symbol for the Chaldean Church

Secret Plan To Build The Third Temple of Solomon

Since the destruction of the Second Temple by the Romans in 70 AD, the Jews have longed for and prayed for the rebuilding of a Third Temple in Jerusalem, on Mount Moriah. Three of the world's major religions worship there—Christians, Jews, and Muslims. The First Temple is said to have been built by King Solomon around 932 BC directly over the Foundation Stone, deep inside the planet.

Of course, a major issue regarding the rebuilding of the Temple is that the Dome of the Rock Mosque and the Al Aqsa Mosque are both there. What to do?

Russian President Putin visited Jerusalem in recent years and said that the Temple should be rebuilt. Israeli Prime Minister Netanyahu has vowed that the Third Temple would be built during his time in office.

Architectural plans for the new Temple building are completed and are on display nearby the Temple Mount. In September 2018 a pure red heifer was born. This is a sign that it is now time for the Third Temple. Many artifacts related to previous temples have been unearthed in recent years, indicating to the rabbis that God is returning all items needed for the Third Temple and religious services.

President Donald Trump has been viewed by religious Jews in Israel as a fulfillment of the prophecy that the descendants of Edom would rebuild the Temple. When President Trump moved the U.S. Embassy to Jerusalem, talk of End Times prophecies was encouraged.

Currently, the government of the Kingdom of Jordan has control over the Temple Mount, even though it is in Israeli territory. This was part of the peace treaty that was arranged between Jordan and Israel.

However, secret negotiations behind the scenes with President Trump, Saudi Arabia, Jewish leaders, and Muslim clerics is designed to transfer the control of the Temple Mount to Saudi Arabia in a sweeping regional peace deal that would also pave the way for a new Temple.

Saudi Arabia and other Arab Gulf nations have been becoming quite friendly lately and all want a new way of life in a peaceful region.

So, how could the Dome of the Rock be removed? War? Earthquake? Agreement with Muslims? Something else? We will know soon enough.

In Hebrew Gematria, Donald Trump = 424.

Messiah for the House of David = 424.

Interesting!

Historical and prophetic Temple facts

- Persian King Cyrus destroyed Babylon 2500 years ago and allowed the Jews to return to Jerusalem to rebuild the Temple. President Trump has been compared to King Cyrus and the Israelis even minted a coin with both their faces on it.

- The Zohar states that in 2012-2013, the Messiah was secretly presented to Rabbis in Israel. At that same time Rabbinic Authorities told students not to leave Israel because the Messiah was already there.

- Rabbi Judah ben Samuel in Germany in 1217 predicted the rising of the Ottoman Empire and said that 2017 begins the Messianic Era.

- Many Muslim scholars believe it is time for the Third Temple.

- Most Latin American countries believe that the Jews should build the Third Temple.

- Saudi Arabia wants Jordan removed from control of the Temple Mount and says that the so-called Palestinians need to change their views.

- The Torah states that after the Temple is built, someone named "Armilus" would deceive the world into idol worship.

- God says throughout the Bible that His Covenant to give Israel to the Jews is everlasting and eternal.

- God says that the territory of Israel should extend from the desert to Lebanon to the Euphrates River to the Great Sea/Mediterranean Sea, and all Hittite country/Turkey and Syria.

- The Sanhedrin/Supreme Court of Israel has artifacts in place to start Temple services.

- Ethiopian Jews believe that the Ark of the Covenant is in Axum, Ethiopia, brought by Menelik l, son of Queen Sheba and King Solomon.

- The Ark was removed to Israel during the Falasha Jews airlift of the late 1980s.

- The Bible says that the King of Judah, Rehoboamk, gave the Ark to Egyptian Pharoah Shisak, to prevent the destruction of Jerusalem. (Could there be replica Arks?)

- But, 200+ years later, King Josiah ordered the return of the Ark to the Temple.

- The Copper Scroll discovered in Qumran cave in 1952 lists 64 locations to find gold and silver items.

- The Copper Scroll indicates that the Ark is hidden in Mt. Nebo, now in Jordan.

- There is controversy over the exact location of the Temple. Some Jewish researchers say it was in the City of David, not on Mt. Moriah. That would be about 600 feet/200 meters from the Dome of the Rock. However, the Bible clearly states that the Temple was located on Mt. Moriah.

- The prophecy of the Temple being rebuilt by descendants of Edom means non-Jews will build it.

- Earthquakes and pestilence mark the beginning of Tribulation, including nations rising against nations. (This is certainly happening!)

- Fundamentalist Christians believe that Jesus will return after the Third Temple is built. Then, Christ will build a Fourth Temple.

- After the Third Temple is built, the laws of Israel revert to ancient ways, thus land will be redistributed to each of the 12 Tribes again.

- New Jerusalem will be in orbit around the Earth. (Giant spaceship?)

- The Antichrist is the "seed of the serpent" (Corrupt Human DNA? See Book of Enoch).

- There will be a Chinese invasion of Asia, the Kings of the East. (Will this be for or against Israel?)

So much to ponder. It is all happening *now*, right in front of your eyes! This is why there are so many billions of people on Earth. Everyone came to witness and participate in this unique experience of God-Mind.

The Revelation of The Messiah, by the Chief Rabbi of Israel

In 2005, Orthodox Rabbi Yitzchak Kaduri, Chief Rabbi of Israel, claimed he met the true Messiah. He wrote a note in code with the name to be revealed after his death. Rabbi Kaduri died in 2006 at the age of 108 years old.

His orders were to keep the note sealed until one year after his death. In 2007, exactly one year after his passing, the note was opened, decoded and read:

Yehoshua/Yeshua is the name of the real Messiah—Jesus!

Of course, his family and friends, as well as many Israelis, claimed it was a fraud and a hoax. They wanted the note destroyed.

Kaduri's close students believed him. So did the Christians who support the Jews and Israel, called, B'nei Noach—Sons of Noah. Even Prime Minister Netanyahu has studied this information.

Kabalistic rabbis knew that the Messiah could only appear after the death of former Prime Minister Ariel Sharon, who was in a coma at that time. It was rumored that the Kabalistic rabbis had performed an Aramaic curse on Sharon called Pulsa Denura/Lashing of Fire. They did this because they were against his domestic and foreign policies, which the Orthodox Jews said hurt Judaism and prevented the Messiah from coming.

After a while, the information about the note from Rabbi Kaduri vanished from the Internet. The note said that Yeshua was the Aleph and Tav/Alpha and Omega.

Consider the symbolisms:

Ancient Hebrew		**Modern Hebrew**		
Beginning	ᚻ	Aleph	א	= Al = God
Ending	†	Tav	ת	= Tov = Good

In ancient times, the symbol for "end" and "good" was the cross.

In those days, Mary said Jesus had no human father. The rabbis therefore referred to him as a *mamzer*/bastard and said that he was never to marry a Jew. He was given the acronym "Yeshu." Yeshu are letters that stand for "May his name be forgotten."

Yeshua is a play on words.

Yeshua/Jesus was called the derogatory name of "Yeshu ben Pantera," meaning "Yeshu, son of the Panther."

He was called this because it was believed his real father was a Roman soldier named Pantera believed to be Mary's lover.

In addition:

- The Apostle Paul used Kabalistic terms in his writings.

- Jesus/Yeshua also used Kabalistic terms.

- The Thomas Code is based on Kabballah.

- Ariel Sharon died in 2014. That is when the rabbis told their students to remain in Israel.

- Kaduri's real name was "Yitzchak Diba" and he was born in Baghdad.

- When the Ottoman Turks came to Iraq recruiting soldiers for WWI, Diba escaped with Holy Scrolls to Jerusalem. There he changed his name to Kaduri, a Kabalistic word meaning "Sphere."

- In the Old Testament, Isaiah says that help for Israel would come from Sinim/China. Is this the Chinese invasion from prophecy? The Children of the East?

- By 2030, China will have the largest Christian population on Earth.
- Kaduri's note was read by 15+ million Chinese on the Internet.
- In May 2018, The Sanhedrin Court said that the time has come to rebuild the Temple on Mount Moriah in Jerusalem. A letter stating this was also sent to all high level Muslim Imams.
- Yeshua = Salvation from God; Jmmanuel = God is with us.
- Are Yeshua and Jmmanuel two different terms that mean the same?
- It is widely believed by Christians and Jewish Messianic believers that Isaiah 53 is about Yeshua/Jesus/Messiah. Read it for yourself and then you decide!

Isaiah 53 New International Version (NIV)

53 Who has believed our message
   and to whom has the arm of the LORD been revealed?
² He grew up before him like a tender shoot,
   and like a root out of dry ground.
He had no beauty or majesty to attract us to him,
   nothing in his appearance that we should desire him.
³ He was despised and rejected by mankind,
   a man of suffering, and familiar with pain.
Like one from whom people hide their faces
   he was despised, and we held him in low esteem.
⁴ Surely he took up our pain
   and bore our suffering,
yet we considered him punished by God,
   stricken by him, and afflicted.
⁵ But he was pierced for our transgressions,
   he was crushed for our iniquities;
the punishment that brought us peace was on him,
   and by his wounds we are healed.

⁶ We all, like sheep, have gone astray,
    each of us has turned to our own way;
and the Lord has laid on him
    the iniquity of us all.
⁷ He was oppressed and afflicted,
    yet he did not open his mouth;
he was led like a lamb to the slaughter,
    and as a sheep before its shearers is silent,
    so he did not open his mouth.
⁸ By oppression and judgment he was taken away.
    Yet who of his generation protested?
For he was cut off from the land of the living;
    for the transgression of my people he was punished.]
⁹ He was assigned a grave with the wicked,
    and with the rich in his death,
though he had done no violence,
    nor was any deceit in his mouth.
¹⁰ Yet it was the Lord's will to crush him and cause him to suffer,
    and though the Lord makes his life an offering for sin,
he will see his offspring and prolong his days,
    and the will of the Lord will prosper in his hand.
¹¹ After he has suffered,
    he will see the light of life and be satisfied;
by his knowledge my righteous servant will justify many,
    and he will bear their iniquities.
¹² Therefore I will give him a portion among the great,
    and he will divide the spoils with the strong,
because he poured out his life unto death,
    and was numbered with the transgressors.
For he bore the sin of many,
    and made intercession for the transgressors.

I think it is.

Koshering of Humanity

There is a koshering of humanity happening right now.

When meat is koshered, it is soaked in a large pot of salt water that allows all the congealed, contaminated blood to leak out. Then, the salt water is dumped and the meat is rinsed in fresh water. The meat is repeatedly soaked until no more blood comes out. The meat is thus purified, cleansed, and ready to use.

Humanity is being cleansed now; it is being, "koshered."

Moses parted the salt water of the Red Sea so the people could pass. Then the Egyptian army was drowned as the salt water flooded back, koshering them. When the people of Israel arrived at the fresh water of the Jordan River before entering the Holy Land, they were immersed therein and thus, koshered.

Finally, Christ represented the symbolic koshering of humanity via the letting of His blood. When the spear was thrust in his side, water also came out. Blood and water = koshering.

Today, during this End Times process, Human Beings are being changed and contaminated via their blood. Drugs, alcohol, synthetic pot, narcotics, poisoned food, and prescriptions, along with the contaminants in the air and water, all contribute to the degradation of Humankind.

Human blood needs to be cleaned. Human bodies are 70% water that needs to be cleaned. Humans need to eliminate the demons and astral entities that control them and return to the pure state of Being, as God-Mind intended.

Writings of Ari

Rabbi Isaac Luria (1534-1572) was known as the Ari/Lion. Until his lifetime, no one was able to properly understand the depths of the Zohar. Without his explanations, the Zohar does not make sense.

His work is known as the *Kitvey Ari*, or "Writings of Ari." His main work is called *Pri Etz Chaim*, or "Fruit of the Tree of Life." This explains many things about the Sefirot/Tree of Life. Most importantly, this explains how to apply what is in the Zohar.

The Ari also wrote *Shemoneh Shearim*, or "Eight Gates." They describes as follows:

First Gate: Gates of Introduction and theoretical information.

Second Gate: The Gate of Zoharic Teachings.

Third Gate: The Gate of Talmudic Teachings.

Fourth Gate: The Gate of Biblical Verses.

Fifth Gate: The Gate of the Commandments.

Sixth Gate: The Gate of Meditations.

Seventh Gate: Gate of Divine Inspirations that describes how to use the Ari's system as a meditation.

Eighth Gate: Gate of Reincarnations.

His work also says that there are three types of Kaballah:

Theoretical = Descriptions of the spiritual realms

Meditative = Tells you how to get into inner space.

Practical also known as Magical = There are almost no books in print on this topic. The main book on this topic is called *Shoshan Yesod Olam,* or "Rose Foundation of the World." There is only one known manuscript in Existence.

The following are some key points in his work:

- In the Tetragrammaton, YHVH, the four letters are meaningful because each is related to the verb "to be." In Hebrew, *Hayah* means "was," *Hoveh* means "is," and *Yiyeh* means "will be." Therefore understanding the YHVH means that God was, is, and will be.

- The "crown" on top of the Yud in the Tetragrammaton is called, *Yechidah*. This word comes from the word *Echad*/one, and leads to *Yichid*/unity. Yichud is related to Yehud/Jew.

- The iterations from Tzimtzum that create the "5 Levels of Creation" also produce decreasing levels of awareness and increasing levels of concealment. This is why in Hebrew, the word for Universe/World is *Olam* and the word for concealing is *Alam*.

- Sandalphon, one of the Super-Angelic Beings, has a purpose. The name comes from Sandal/shoe and Phon, from the Ophanim/wheel angels. Wheel means spinning or turning like a vortex. Therefore, Sandalphon has a function of connecting the physical to the spiritual and works together with Metatron as a collective high spiritual consciousness.

- The Sefirot are said to be 5 sets of opposites. Sefirot is related to the word *Sefer*/book. Therefore, the Sefirot are centers for information.

- The Absolute is referred to as *Ain Sof*/without end. Infinity. *Ain*/nothing, without. *Ani*/I am. By switching the letters, I am = Nothingness.
- In some Kabalistic circles, the Keter is excluded from being part of the Sefirot because it is the Crown and above the actual body. Instead, this is replaced with Da'at/pineal gland. This implies that you cannot *know* God's Will, represented by the Keter/Crown. But, you can understand the Da'at, which means Knowing and allows Free Choice. This explains the difference between Free Will/only part of the God-Mind vs. Free Choice, which comes from the decisions made by Humans.
- The Kabballah explains the true meanings of words so you can understand Creation. The two Sefirot, *Chokhmah*/Wisdom and *Binah*/Understanding, are to either side of *Da'at*/Knowing.
- Chokhmah is related to the past; Binah is related to the future. Da'at is the present moment. This tells you that you derive wisdom from the past so that you know the present situation so you can understand the future/what is coming.
- The Hebrew word for "male" is *Zachar,* which also means "to remember." Male energy relates to the past.
- The Hebrew word for "female" is *Nekevah*, which comes from the root "*Nikev,*" meaning "to pierce."
- This explains the need for physical sexual intercourse where the male "pierces" the female, recreating the act of Tzimtzum, which creates orgasm.
- The Zohar states that Adam was created already circumcised; the perfect template of origin. However, the sins committed in Eden made the foreskin appear and cover the symbol of Tzimtzum, the Initiation of Creation.
- This can be interpreted as part of the corruption of Humankind when the mammalian genetics were mixed with the Reptilian

DNA and the foreskin appeared. In Kabballah, the foreskin is a symbol of evil works.

- The Sefirot are also alluded to as vessels that hold the Light of God. However, God's light is so powerful, the vessels break and that is what manifests in physical reality as evil…broken "vessels" that need to be repaired.

- This, then, is what created the need for *Tikkun*/rectification, or, the reorganizing of the Chaos/Void that refills the vessels with light and returns all to perfection as originally intended. This explains the entire purpose of all Physical Realities.

When you study the Torah, Kabballah, and Zohar, you must be prepared for intense explanations, multiple versions, and the need to mentally conceive the information, rather than consigning them to human words. You can study each Sefirah for a lifetime and still not learn all of the levels and symbolisms.

Since the Absolute and God-Mind are Infinite, so is all Creation. As above, so below. This is why you have infinite lifetimes in infinite realities to learn and rediscover your Self. In so doing, you correct all corruptions. You enhance Creation and bring pleasure to the Creator.

The Teachings That Cannot Be Taught

Writing and researching these three books in this series was perhaps the most intense and mind-expanding work I have ever done. There were times when I wanted to stop and walk away. Every layer led me to more deep and powerful information for which human words were inadequate.

As I studied and read, there was so much more I could have included. But then I would never be finished. There was always more and more. I had to draw the line. Truthfully, I prefer to disseminate this information in a class, face-to-face. This knowledge is not meant to be written or given to the general public who would misuse it and not understand. This is why Zohar and Kaballah were not allowed to be taught until the 19th Century. This is why it is often referred to as "The teachings that cannot be taught."

In the time it took me to create these volumes, many positive changes occurred in my life. For me, it is a proof of the power of this knowledge.

One of my most incredible discoveries is that of an image in a book on secret Kaballah that shows a dove with a sword and a leaf in its mouth! That is my name—Sverdlov—the sword and the leaf!

In addition, to be married to a woman with the maiden name of Mourglia, directly connected to Mount Moriah in Jerusalem, goes beyond normal circumstances.

courtesy of author Joel David Bakst © 2006

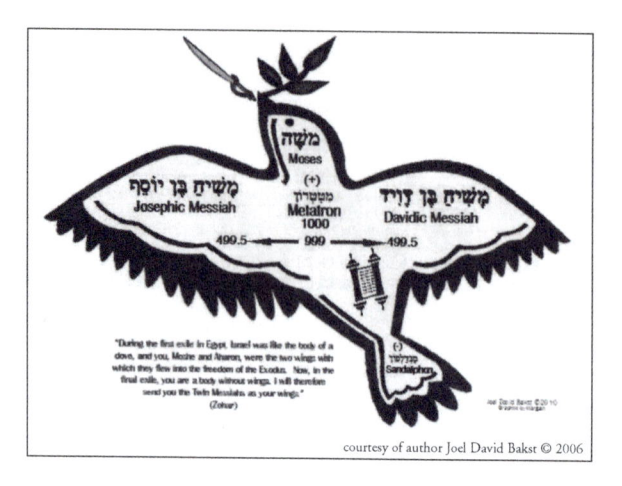

We are living in the real End Times. And it is *real*. Now is the time for all of this to emerge to the public, ready or not! Here it comes!

This time in history will be recorded as the greatest spiritual war in this Solar System and specifically on Earth. We live on a Mother World. We have a Foundation Stone. This is a Holy Planet.

It is up to you now. Choose properly. There is no time left to ponder and waste. We are on the edge of a new world of love, peace, and hope…or destruction and slavery.

Which will *you* choose?

Appendices

72 Names of God

The ancient Kabbalist Rav Shimon bar Yochai wrote in the *Zohar* that it was Moses, not God, who parted the Red Sea, allowing the Israelites to narrowly escape Pharaoh and the Egyptian army. In order to accomplish this miracle, Moses combined the power of certainty with a very powerful spiritual technology. He had possession of a formula that literally gave him access to the subatomic realm of nature.

The formula Moses used to overcome the laws of nature has been hidden in the *Zohar* for 2000 years.

This formula is called the 72 Names of God. Not names like Betty, Bill and Barbara, but rather 72 sequences composed of Hebrew letters that have the extraordinary power to overcome the laws of nature in all forms, including human nature.

Though this formula is encoded in the literal Biblical story of the parting of the Red Sea, no rabbi, scholar, or priest was aware of the secret. It was known only to a handful of kabbalists - who also knew that when the time was right, the formula would be revealed to the world.

To learn how to wield the power of the 72 Names, together with the purposes of which they can be used, we recommend reading *The 72 Names of God: Technology of the Soul*. Even if you don't speak or read Hebrew, you can still begin and experience incredible miracles.

Now, after some 2,000 years of concealment, contemporary seekers can also tap into this power and energy by learning about, and calling upon, the 72 Names of God.

The 72 Names are each 3-letter sequences that act like an index to specific, spiritual frequencies. By simply looking at the letters, as well as closing your eyes and visualizing them, you can connect with these frequencies.

To use a physical metaphor to describe what takes place when using the 72 Names, think of a tuning fork, a tool used to establish a precise pitch. When you bring a vibrating tuning fork close to another tuning fork that is not vibrating, the second fork starts to vibrate by the phenomena called 'sympathetic transference'.

The 72 Names work as tuning forks to repair you on the soul level. It means, practically speaking, that you don't have to go through some of the more physically demanding tests in life; you can tune your body and soul with the spiritual frequencies your eyes do not perceive.

72 Vortices

In the Torah, Kabballah, and Zohar, it is stated that there are 72 names of God. These are based on the combination possibilities of the master formula YHVH.

Correspondingly on this planet, there are 72 vortices that are both natural and humanmade. There are many more than just these. However, these are the ones most concerning.

The Illuminati/evil ones have a plan to open these vortices to allow hordes of demonic entities upon the Earth to control humans.

Some of these vortices have already been opened. Some have been blocked. This is part of the process of the spiritual war of End Times.

The 72 locations are as follows:
- Stonehenge/Salisbury/Avebury
- Notre Dame, France
- Yellowstone
- Taupo, NZ
- Temple Mount
- Giza Plateau
- Easter Island
- Washington Monument
- Capitol Building WA DC

- Empire State Building
- Bermuda Triangle
- Devil's Triangle
- Lake Michigan Triangle
- Marianna Trench
- Caribbean Trench
- North Pole
- South Pole
- Mt. Rainier/Seattle
- Mt. St. Helens
- Pompeii
- Vatican
- Mecca
- Jericho
- Parthenon
- Lhasa Monastery
- Hiroshima
- Nagasaki
- Forbidden City, China
- Buckingham Palace
- Balmoral Castle
- Mormon Temple
- Luxor
- Las Vegas
- Hollywood
- World Trade Center
- Montauk Point
- Camelback Mountain

- CERN
- Devil's Tower, Wyoming
- Disney World, Florida
- Disneyland, California
- Louvre, France
- Big Island, Hawaii
- El Yunque, Puerto Rico
- Salton Sea, Mexico
- Uluru, Australia
- Popocatepetl, Mexico
- Zona de Silencio, Mexico
- Taos
- Tiahuanaco
- Malta
- Canary Islands
- Lake Baikal
- Caspian Sea
- Black Sea
- Mt. Hermon
- Mt. Everest
- Mt. McKinley
- UN Headquarters Building, New York
- Baghdad
- Mt. Ararat
- Bosnian Pyramids
- Crimea
- Taj Mahal
- Sydney Opera House

- Mt. Krakatoa
- Hekla/Katla Volcanoes
- Ellesmere Island, Canada
- New Orleans, Lousiana
- Carnac, France
- Rift Valley, East Africa

Minor Vortices

- Ozarks
- Smokey Mountains
- Altai Mountains
- Kyoto
- Bali

The 72 Names of God with Functions

#	Name	Function
1	Vav Hey Vav	Time Travel
2	Yud Lamed Yud	Recapturing the Sparks
3	Tet Yud Samech	Miracle Making
4	Mem Lamed Ayin	Eliminating Negative Thoughts
5	Shin Hey Mem	Healing
6	Hey Lamed Lamed	Dream State
7	Aleph Kaf Aleph	DNA of The Soul
8	Tav Hey Kaf	Defusing Negative Energy
9	Yud Zayin Hey	Angelic Influences
10	Daled Lamed Aleph	Protection from Evil Eye
11	Vav Aleph Lamed	Banishing the Remnants of Evil
12	Ayin Hey Hey	Unconditional Love
13	Lamed Zayin Yud	Heaven on Earth
14	Hey Bet Mem	Farewell to Arms
15	Yud Resh Hey	Long Range Vision
16	Mem Kuf Hey	Dumping Depression
17	Vav Aleph Lamed	Great Escape
18	Yud Lamed Kaf	Fertility
19	Vav Vav Lamed	Dialing God
20	Lamed Hey Pey	Victory over Addictions
21	Kaf Lamed Nun	Eradicate Plague
22	Yud Yud Yud	Stop Fatal Attraction
23	Hey Lamed Mem	Sharing the Flame
24	Vav Hey Chet	Jealousy
25	Hey Tav Nun	Speak Your Mind
26	Aleph Aleph Hey	Order From Chaos
27	Tav Resh Yud	Silent Partner
28	Hey Aleph Shin	Soulmate
29	Yud Yud Resh	Removing Hatred
30	Mem Vav Aleph	Building Bridges
31	Bet Kaf Lamed	Finish What You Start
32	Resh Shin Vav	Memories
33	Vav Chet Yud	Revealing the Dark Side
34	Chet Hey Lamed	Forget Thyself
35	Kuf Vav Kaf	Sexual Energy
36	Daled Nun Mem	Fear(Less)
37	Yud Nun Aleph	The Big Picture
38	Mem Ayin Chet	Circuitry
39	Ayin Hey Resh	Diamond in the Rough
40	Zayin Yud Yud	Speaking the Right Words
41	Hey Hey Hey	Self Esteem
42	Kaf Yud Mem	Revealing the Concealed
43	Lamed Vav Vav	Defying Gravity
44	Hey Lamed Yud	Sweetening Judgment
45	Lamed Aleph Samech	Power of Prosperity
46	Yud Resh Ayin	Absolute Certainty
47	Lamed Shin Ayin	Global Transformation
48	Hey Yud Yud	Unity
49	Vav Hey Vav	Happiness
50	Yud Nun Daled	Enough is Never Enough
51	Shin Chet Hey	No Guilt
52	Mem Mem Ayin	Passion
53	Aleph Nun Nun	No Agenda
54	Tav Yud Nun	Death of Death
55	Hey Bet mem	Thought Into Action
56	Yud Vav Pey	Dispelling Anger
57	Mem Mem Nun	Listening to Your Soul
58	Lamed Yud Yud	Letting Go
59	Chet Resh Hey	Umbilical Cord
60	Resh Zadik Mem	Freedom
61	Bet Mem Vav	Water
62	Hey Hey Yud	Parent-Teacher, Not Preacher
63	Vav Nun Ayin	Appreciation
64	Yud Chet Mem	Casting Yourself in a Favorable Light
65	Bet Mem Daled	Fear of God
66	Kuf Nun Mem	Accountability
67	Ayin Yud Aleph	Great Expectations
68	Vav Bet Chet	Contacting Departed Souls
69	Hey Aleph Resh	Lost & Found
70	Mem Bet Yud	Design Beneath Disorder
71	Yud Yud Hey	Prophecy & Parallel Universes
72	Mem Vav Mem	Spiritual Cleansing

Names for God

Hebrew Name	English Meaning	Scripture
El-Elyon	God Most High	Gen. 14:18,22
El-Kanna	Jealous	Exod. 34:14
El-Olam	Eternal God	Gen. 21:33
El-Shaddai	God Almighty	Gen. 17:1
Jehovah (YHWH)	The LORD	Exod. 6:2–3
Jehovah-Adon Kal Ha'arets	Lord of All the Earth	Josh. 3:13
Jehovah-Bara	Creator	Isa. 40:28
Jehovah-Chereb	Glorious Sword	Deut. 33:29
Jehovah-Eli	My God	Ps. 18:2
Jehovah-Elohenu	Our God	Exod. 8:10
Jehovah-Gibbor Milchamah	Mighty in Battle	Ps. 24:8
Jehovah-Go'el	Redeemer	Isa. 49:26; 60:16
Jehovah-Hamelech	The King	Ps. 98:6
Jehovah-Hashopet	The Judge	Judg. 11:27
Jehovah-Hoshe'ah	The LORD Who Saves	Ps. 20:9
Jehovah-'Izuz 'Gibbor	Strong and Mighty	Ps. 24:8
Jehovah-Jireh	The LORD Will Provide	Gen. 22:14
Jehovah-Kabodhi	My Glory	Ps. 3:3
Jehovah-Keren-Yish'i	Horn of My Salvation	Ps. 18:2
Jehovah-Machsi	My Refuge	Ps. 91:9
Jehovah-Magen	The Shield	Deut. 33:29
Jehovah-Makeh	The LORD Who Strikes You	Ezek. 7:9
Jehovah-Ma'ozi	My Fortress	Jer. 16:19
Jehovah-Mekoddishkem	The LORD Who Makes You Holy	Exod. 31:13
Jehovah-Melech 'Olam	King Forever	Ps. 10:16
Jehovah-Mephalti	My Deliverer	Ps. 18:2
Jehovah-Moshi'ech	Your Savior	Isa. 49:26; 60:16
Jehovah-Nissi	My Banner	Exod. 17:15
Jehovah-'Ori	My Light	Ps. 27:1
Jehovah-Rohi	My Shepherd	Ps. 23:1
Jehovah-Rophe	The LORD Who Heals You	Exod. 15:26
Jehovah-Sabaoth	The LORD of Hosts	1 Sam. 1:3
Jehovah-Sel'i	My Rock	Ps. 18:2
Jehovah-Tsidkenu	Our Righteousness	Jer. 32:6
Jehovah-Uzi	My Strength	Ps. 28:7

The Seventy-Two Living Divine Names of the Most High
Instructions for Using the 72 Names of God

First, sit in a comfortable chair with your palms up in a dark room, Then get into a meditative zone and quiet your mind, gently pushing out any extraneous thoughts. Begin to do slow rhythmic breathing and focus on your third eye...Think of this as a computer software program for the evolution of your soul. You are about to utilize a powerful code to access very specific energies for soul correction and transformation. Begin by studying the chart of the 72 Names of God to see what aspects of your life are in need of a spiritual boost. If you are spiritual attuned, you will automatically resonate with a particular name and meaning that your soul knows is for your highest good and needs immediate attending to.

After you have identified which name you wish to meditate on, click with your computer mouse until the box expands to reveal a larger version of the holy name and spiritual intention you have chosen to meditate on. To further facilitate your meditation, you may opt to add a selection of soothing trance music or nature sounds by clicking on one of the selections provided in the audio player below the expanded box...or ignore it and do the meditation in silence.

1. Ask permission of the Light to use the holy Hebrew letters for your meditative purpose. Since God created the worlds with these letters they are holy and belong to him.

2. Be humble but direct as you state your intention. Call upon the Lightforce of God for what you specifically wish to accomplish through this meditation. For example, if the purpose is to transform negative emotions to their positive counterparts, list these emotions in your own words. Ask that the healing energy from the specific name of God help to transform these negative emotions.

3. Begin again with slow and rhythmic deep breathing. Gently push away any extraneous thoughts so that you may completely concentrate only on your breath. As you drift into an alpha state, imagine that the three letter combination of Hebrew letters are brightly smoldering as if on fire. All the illusions of existence begin to fade off and you are alone with your thoughts as never before...You are alone with the Lightforce of God. Begin to repeat like a mantra, slowly over and over again, the English transliteration of the Hebrew letters. If possible, vibrate the letters at the pitch of middle C. You will begin to develop a slow rhythmic breathing cadence of repeating the letters over and over again in a manner that is comfortable for you. As your meditation on the holy three letter name of God and the angel behind becomes more intense, the letters will glow brighter and brighter.

4. Start with 5 minutes a day and try to work up to 20 minutes a day. As you bring yourself out of the meditation, remember to sit for two minutes to completely come back from alpha state.

5. With consistent practice you will, over time, get more advanced in your meditation. Your intentions will grow more complicated, you may want to combine two names together. This would involve a "stitching process" whereby you create a new hybridized name. This occurs in the following manner: take the first letter from the first name with the first letter of the second name, the second letter of the first name with the second letter of the second name, and the third letter of the first name with the third letter of the second name. Repeat this new six-letter name as a mantra over and over again as you would the three-letter name.

Decoding the Holy Names and Their Supernal Meaning

Before you begin this powerful meditation, it is important to understand how the Hebrew prophets and rabbis that were steeped in Kabbalah, used this coded toolset to slip into altered states of consciousness. The source for deriving the 72 Names of God and the angel that is behind each name is derived by using a specific formula for letter combinations that comes from the letters contained in Verses 19, 20, & 21 from Chapter 14 from Parashat Beshalach from the Book of Shemot (Exodus) from the Torah. Each of these three verses contains 72 letters. Collectively they describe the peak moments of the splitting of the Red Sea.

19 And the angel of God, which went before the camp of Israel, removed and went behind them; and the pillar of the cloud went from before their face, and stood behind them: 20 And it came between the camp of the Egyptians and the camp of Israel; and it was a cloud and darkness to them, but it gave light by night to these: so that the one came not near the other all the night. 21 And Moses stretched out his hand over the sea; and the Lord caused the sea to go back by a strong east wind all that night, and made the sea dry land, and the waters were divided.

The formula for a three-letter combination is constructed in the following manner: take the first letter from Verse 19 and then combine it with the last letter from Verse 20 and the first letter from Verse 21. The second three-letter combination is obtained by taking the second letter from Verse 19, combining it with the second to last letter from Verse 20, and the second letter from Verse 21 and so on. This process is continued until a total of 72 three-letter combinations are formed. Each three-letter combination is the name of a specific attribute of God as well as being the name of a specific angel that represents that attribute of God.

The combination of these 72 names creates a 216-letter name of God, that is commonly referred to as the Shemhamphorasch or Shem ha-Mephorash. As referenced in Exodus 23:20-21, it states:

"Behold, I send an angel before you, to guard you on the way and to bring you to the place which I have prepared. Give heed to him and hearken to his voice, do not rebel against him, for he will not pardon your transgressions; for my name is in him."

This specifically refers to Archangel Michael who is represented by a three - letter name of God - #51 on the chart, which is pronounced "Nun Nun Aleph". The gematria of this is 101, which is also the gematria of the letters Mem, Yud, Caf, Aleph, Lamed which make up the word Michael. (Gematria is a Kabbalistic system where each Hebrew letter has an equivalent mathematical value. This hidden system is used to deduce hidden supernal meanings where the gematria of one word is equal to the gematria of another word, and therefore the literal meaning of that same word.) Michael collectively "presides" over all of the other angels involved in this collective endeavor as well.

Now that you have a basic Kabbalistic understanding of how the 72 Names of God were derived, you are ready to partake of this amazing meditation tool.

Em Hebraico	Anjo	Signo	Planeta	Em Hebraico	Anjo	Signo	Planeta
והויה	1. VEHUIAH	♌	Saturno ♄	אניאל	37. ANIEL	♒	Vênus ♀
יליאל	2. JELIEL	♌	Saturno ♄	חעמיה	38. HAAMIAH	♒	Vênus ♀
סיטאל	3. SITAEL	♌	Júpiter ♃	רהעאל	39. REHAEL	♒	Mercúrio ☿
עלמיה	4. ELEMIAH	♌	Júpiter ♃	ייזאל	40. IEIAZEL	♒	Mercúrio ☿
מהשיה	5. MAHASIAH	♌	Marte ♂	ההחאל	41. HAHAHEL	♒	Lua ☾
ללהאל	6. LELAHEL	♌	Marte ♂	מיכאל	42. MIKAEL	♒	Lua ☾
אכאיה	7. AKAIAH	♍	Sol ☉	וליה	43. VEUALIAH	♓	Saturno ♄
כהתאל	8. CAHETEL	♍	Sol ☉	ילהיה	44. IELAHIAH	♓	Saturno ♄
הזיאל	9. HAZIEL	♍	Vênus ♀	סאליה	45. SEALIAH	♓	Júpiter ♃
אלדיה	10. ALADIAH	♍	Vênus ♀	עריאל	46. ARIEL	♓	Júpiter ♃
לאויה	11. LAUVIAH	♍	Mercúrio ☿	עשליה	47. ASALIAH	♓	Marte ♂
ההעיה	12. HAHAIAH	♍	Mercúrio ☿	מיהאל	48. MIHAEL	♓	Marte ♂
יזלאל	13. IEZALEL	♎	Lua ☾	והואל	49. VEHUEL	♈	Marte ♂
מבהאל	14. MEBAHEL	♎	Lua ☾	דניאל	50. DANIEL	♈	Marte ♂
הריאל	15. HARIEL	♎	Saturno ♄	החשיה	51. HAHASIAH	♈	Sol ☉
הקמיה	16. HAKAMIAH	♎	Saturno ♄	עממ	52. IMAMIAH	♈	Sol ☉
לאויה	17. LAUVIAH	♎	Júpiter ♃	נגאאל	53. NANAEL	♈	Vênus ♀
כליאל	18. CALIEL	♎	Júpiter ♃	ניתאל	54. NITHAEL	♈	Vênus ♀
לויה	19. LEUVIAH	♏	Marte ♂	מבהיה	55. MEBAIAH	♉	Mercúrio ☿
פהליה	20. PAHALIAH	♏	Marte ♂	פויאל	56. POIEL	♉	Mercúrio ☿
נלכאל	21. NELCHAEL	♏	Sol ☉	נממיה	57. NEMAMIAH	♉	Lua ☾
ייי	22. IEIAIEL	♏	Sol ☉	יילאל	58. IEIALEL	♉	Lua ☾
מלהאל	23. MELAHEL	♏	Vênus ♀	הרחאל	59. HARAHEL	♉	Saturno ♄
חהויה	24. HAHIUIAH	♏	Vênus ♀	מצראל	60. MITZRAEL	♉	Saturno ♄
נתהיה	25. NITH HAIAH	♐	Mercúrio ☿	ומבאל	61. UMABEL	♊	Júpiter ♃
האאיה	26. HAAIAH	♐	Mercúrio ☿	יההאל	62. IAHHEL	♊	Júpiter ♃
ירתאל	27. IERATHEL	♐	Lua ☾	ענואל	63. ANAUEL	♊	Marte ♂
שאהיה	28. SEEHIAH	♐	Lua ☾	מחיאל	64. MEHIEL	♊	Marte ♂
רייאל	29. REIIEL	♐	Saturno ♄	דמביה	65. DAMABIAH	♊	Sol ☉
אומאל	30. OMAEL	♐	Saturno ♄	מנקאל	66. MANAKEL	♊	Sol ☉
לכבאל	31. LECABEL	♑	Júpiter ♃	איעאל	67. EIAEL	♋	Vênus ♀
ושריה	32. VASARIAH	♑	Júpiter ♃	חביה	68. HABUIAH	♋	Vênus ♀
יחויה	33. IEHUIAH	♑	Marte ♂	ראהאל	69. ROCHEL	♋	Mercúrio ☿
להחיה	34. LEHAHIAH	♑	Marte ♂	יבמיה	70. JABAMIAH	♋	Mercúrio ☿
כוקיה	35. CHAVAKIAH	♑	Sol ☉	הייאל	71. HAIAIEL	♋	Lua ☾
מנדאל	36. MENADEL	♑	Sol ☉	מום	72. MUMIAH	♋	Lua ☾

Names of 72 Angels Correlated to 72 Names of God

Hebrew Alphabet Chart

Book Print	Name	Block	Cursive	Pronounced	Transliteration
א	Aleph	א	ic	silent letter	' (or none)
בּ	Bet	ב	ɔ	b as in boy	b
ב	Vet	ב	ɔ	*no dot:* v as in vine	v
ג	Gimmel	λ	¿	g as in girl	g
ד	Dalet	ד	ʒ	d as in door	d
ה	Hey	ה	ɔ	h as in hay	h
ו	Vav	ו	l	v as in vine; "consonantal vowel"	v
ז	Zayin	ז	ɟ	z as in zebra	z
ח	Chet	ח	∩	ch as in Bach	ch (or ḥ)
ט	Tet	ט	ɢ	t as in time	t (or ṭ)
י	Yod	י	'	y as in yes; "consonantal vowel"	y
כּ	Kaf	כ	ɔ	k as in kite	k
כ	Khaf	כ	ɔ	*no dot:* ch as in bach	kh
ך		ך	ʔ	*sofit form*	
ל	Lamed	ל	ʃ	l as in look	l
מ	Mem	₥	N	m as in mom	m
ם		□	O	*sofit form*	
נ	Nun	נ	J	n as in now	n
ן		ן	l	*sofit form*	
ס	Samekh	▽	O	s as in son	s
ע	'Ayin	ע	ɣ	silent letter	' (or none)
פּ	Pey	פ	ə	p as in park	p
פ	Fey	פ	ə	ph as in phone	ph / f
ף		ף	ʄ	*sofit form*	
צ	Tsade	✗	3	ts as in nuts	ts (or ṣ)
ץ		ץ	ʒ	*sofit form*	
ק	Qof	ק	ρ	q as in queen	q (or k)
ר	Resh	ר	ɔ	r as in rain	r
שׁ	Shin	ש	e	sh as in shy	sh (or š)
שׂ	Sin	ש	e	s as in sun	s (or ś)
ת	Tav	ת	ת	t as in tall	t

Stewart A. Swerdlow • 207

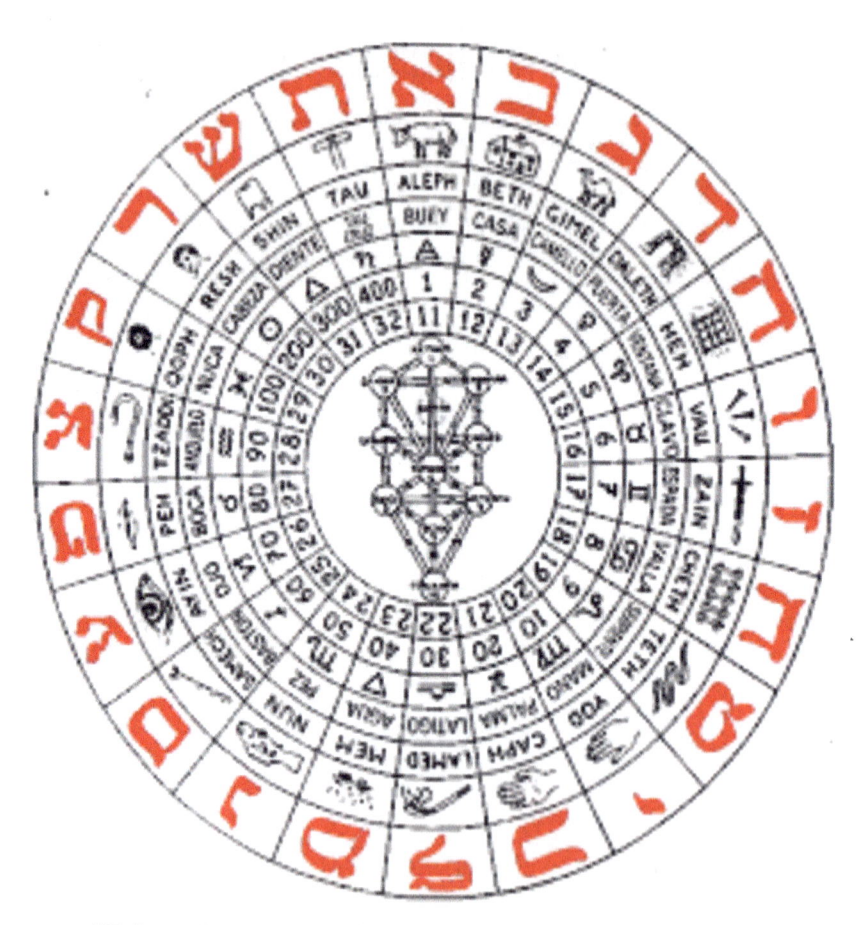

Hebrew Letter Correlation to Astrology and Sephirot

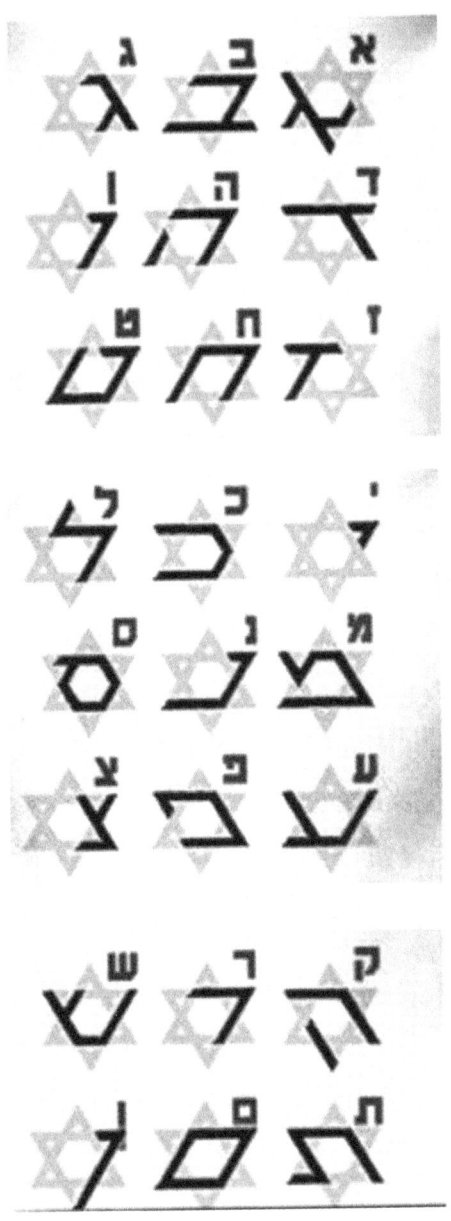

Hebrew Letters From Star of David

210 • Revelations of Time & Space, History and God

Ancient & Mystical Alphabets

Anglo-Roman	Ugaritic Cuneiform	Old Persian Cuneiform	Sumerian Cuneiform	Hieratic	Hieroglyphs	Demotic	Hebrew	Greek	Elder Futhark	Phoenician	Aramaic	Arabic	Brahmi

Glossary

Abba: Father; connected to DMT.
Aggadata: Nonlegal aspects of the Talmud
Ain Sof: Without end; God-Mind.
Anaha: Grief.
Apocrypha: Books removed from the Bible.
Aron Ha Brit: Ark of the Covenant.
Asiyah: Action; lower world.
Beit Ha Mikdash: Holy Temple.
Binah: Understanding.
B'nai: Children.
Bohu: Void.
Chaiyeh: Highest level of the Soul, followed by Neshamah, Ruach, and Nefesh/Lowest level of the Soul.
Chochmah: Wisdom.
Choshech: Darkness.
Chutzpah: Arrogance.
Codex: Levels of symbolic meanings and numerical values.
Da'at: Pineal gland/knowing and knowledge; middle brain.
Davon: Act of praying.
Derech Aitz Chaym: Road to Tree of Life; Spiritual Path.
Drash: Ethics.
Dybbuk: Bad spirit; astral.

Ebion: Poverty.

Even Shetiya: Foundation Stone all reality created, connected to Stonehenge and Macchu Picchu; weaving stone.

Gehinnom: Hell.

Gemara: Amplification and commentary of the Mishnah.

Geonim: Geniuses.

Gilgul: Transmigration of Souls; reincarnation.

Golem: Artificial Intelligence.

Goral/lots: Divination (Urim V'Tumim); using scripture as oracle in Holy Temple on breast plate of Priest.

Halachah: Jewish Law.

Halal: Void.

Hasadim/RT; Gevurot/LT: Divine Masculine/Divine Feminine.

Haskalah: Enlightenment.

Histavut: Balance.

Hitzotzot: Fractal sparks; encoded in Torah.

Imma: Mother; connected to wine.

Kaballah: Receiving.

Kavanot: Mystical intentions.

Keruvim: Cherubs

Keter: Crown

Kishufim: Magic; high technology.

Klal Yisrael: Collective Soul of Israel; Oversoul.

Klipah: Dome.

Klipot: Shells; covering; reference to foreskin.

Kodesh Ha Kedoshim: Holy of Holies; Temple.

Kol Ha Tor: Voice of the Turtle Dove; analysis of Zohar.

Kotel Ha Ma'aravi: Western Wall; Mt. Moriah.

Kudlah/Kudalin: Straight serpent reuniting with self; Kundalini.

Kush: Ethiopia.

Levels of Creation: Atzilut, sparkling white, emanation, Spirit; Beriah, white, creation, thought; Yetzirah, red, formation, feeling; Asiyah, black, corporeal world, action.

Luz: Hazelnut; Pineal Gland (1st Temple, Brainstem, Sod; 2nd Temple Coccyx Bone, Yesod; 3rd Temple Pineal Gland, Pen); connection to Foundation Stone and Lhasa Tibet.

Magid: Spiritual guide.

Makom: The Place; reference to God and Pineal.

Malakh: Angel; messengers.

Malchut: Kingdom.

Mashiach: Mesiah/Twins; Oversoul of ben Yosef/ben David.

Mayim chayim: Living liquid; water.

Mazal: Angel species.

Mazikin: Demon; causes harm to humans.

Merkava: Chariot; energy field of the body.

Midrash: Ancient commentary on Hebrew Scriptures.

Mishnah: Body and codex of the Oral Torah + Gemara.

Mispar: Numbers; root is Sefer-book.

Mitzvah: Good deed.

Nachash: Serpent; king over every other Being.

Nefilim: Giants; hybrids.

Nogah: Glow; spiritual state.

Ohr Ha Ganuz: Hidden light of God-Mind.

Olam Ha Bah: Next world; meet at Pineal.

Olam Ha Zeh: This world; meet at Pineal.

O'rlah: Foreskin.

Pardes: Four dimensions of Torah (Pshat, Remez, Drush, Sod).

Peniel: Face of God.

Prophecy: Kedusha, holiness; Perishah, separation; Hitbo'dedut, isolation.

Pseudepigrapha: Letters, books of Biblical references but never included in the Bible and not verified.

Pshat: Simple narrative.

Rav, Rebbe, Rabbi: Teacher and spiritual leader.

Remez: Intellectual.

Ruach Ha Kodesh: Holy Spirit.

Sar ha Panim: Prince of the face; Metatron.

Sasson, M, Joy/Simcha, F, Happiness: At end of the world they struggle.

Sefer, Book/Sapar, Storyteller/Sippur, the story: How God Created.

Segulot: Ritual spiritual remedies.

Sekhelim Nivdalim: Separate intelligences; angels.

Serafom: Reptilians.

Shadai: Name of God/Sexual; #214 = Metatron.

Shechinah: God's Presence; female.

Shedim: Demons.

Sod: Significant meaning; opposite of Pshat.

Tehom: Abyss.

Talmud: Jewish civil/Mishruh and Ceremonial Law/Gemara.

Talmud: Represents the six orders of Mishnah.

Tefilah: Prayer.

Tefillin: Prayer box; used on forehead.

Teli: Dragon/astral; the Watchers.

Teshuva: Redemption.

Tikun Olam: Rectify/correct personal world.

Tohu: Chaos.

Torah: Instructions; teachings.

Tzedaka: Righteousness; charity.

Tzelem: Aura

Tzimtzum: Contraction that precedes expansion in creation.

Yagon: Sorrow.

Yerushalayim: Jerusalem, city of peace.

Yeshiva: Seminary; religious school.

Yeshua: Jesus/Salvation; not a name.

Yesod: Spinal column

YHVH, called Havaya: Active Being; Being in action; Total Consciousness.

Zion: Location of Foundation Stone; from which all Existence emanates.

Zohar: Splendor, brilliance, radiance.

Index

13-Cubed 4, 56
13-Cubed Squared 4, 56

A

Abba 211
Absolute 3, 7, 9, 13, 14, 132, 134, 138, 139, 141, 142, 146, 191, 192
Abyssinia 78
Adam HaRishon 132
Adam Kadmon 131, 146, 153
African Jews 75
Aggadata 134, 211
Ain Sof 3, 139, 140, 141, 142, 145, 191, 211
Algeria 78
Aliens 4
Anaha 211
Angels 152
Apocrypha 4, 211
Aron Ha Brit 211
Asiyah 153, 211, 213
Assyrians 73
Atlantis 95

B

Babylon 64, 73, 86, 151, 180
Babylonians 73
Bahir 151, 152, 155
Beit Ha Mikdash 211
Berbers 78
Binah 191, 211
Blood 4
Blue Blood, True Blood 4, 95
B'nai 211
Bohu 153, 211

C

Chaiyeh 211
Chesed 136, 146
Chochmah 211
Choshech 211
Chutzpah 211
Cistercian Order 111, 112
Cistercians 9, 112, 114, 115
Codex 211
Creation 4, 13, 14, 29, 132, 136, 138, 139, 141, 145, 146, 153, 190, 191, 192, 213
Creativity 137
Crown Chakra 57
Cube of Space 14–19, 21, 25, 30, 36, 37, 45, 50

D

Da'at 137, 191, 211
Daughters of Zion 64
Davon 211
Decoding Your Life 4
Deprogramming 7
Derech Aitz Chaym 211
DNA 65, 72, 79, 88, 90, 95, 98, 99, 182, 192
Dragon Riders 8
Drash 211
Dybbuk 211

E

Ebion 212
Egalitarianism 137
Egypt 78, 95, 97, 147, 157
End Times 76, 110, 128, 180, 187, 194, 198
Ephraim 66, 68, 72
Esau 81–87, 143, 145
Essenes 9, 90, 104, 112, 113, 115, 151
Ethiopia 74, 78, 115, 181, 213
Even Shetiya 212
Existence 14, 20, 25, 29, 43, 145, 146, 153, 161, 190, 215

F

First Temple 71, 73, 74, 179
Frankists 110

G

Gaon of Vilna 8, 61
Gehinnom 212
Gemara 134, 212, 213, 214
Gematria 72, 98, 133, 145, 146, 161, 180

Geonim 212
Gevurah 136
Gevurot/LT 212
Gilgul 146, 212
God-Mind 3, 4, 7, 9, 13, 14, 72, 89, 111, 112, 114, 133, 137, 138, 145, 162, 182, 188, 191, 192, 211, 213
Golan Heights 72
Golden Dawn 15, 16, 50
Golem 151, 212
Goral 212
Gospel of Thomas 157, 161, 162, 163, 177

H

Halachah 212
Halal 212
Hasadim/RT 212
Haskalah 212
Healer's Handbook 4
Healing 4
Healing Archetypes 4
Healing Archetypes and Symbols 4, 56
Hebrew Gematria 72, 98, 146, 161, 180
Hebrew Tribes 72, 112
Histavut 212
Hitzotzot 212
Holism 137
Hyperspace 4
Hyperspace Helper 4, 56
Hyperspace Plus 4, 56

I

Iberia 111, 112, 113, 116
Igbos 73, 74, 75
Illuminati 110, 198
Imma 212
Inquisition 78, 147
Isaac 81, 83, 84, 85, 145, 189
Israel 8, 63–67, 69, 70, 71, 73, 75–79, 84, 86, 88, 89, 90, 97, 110, 117, 133, 137, 170, 180–184, 187, 212

J

Jacob 65, 66, 75, 81–86, 107, 109
Jerusalem 8, 9, 67, 71, 73, 86, 87, 88, 101, 102, 103, 113, 179, 180–185, 193, 215
Jordan 72, 86, 110, 180, 181, 182, 187
Joseph 1, 2
Judah 66, 68, 72, 73, 74, 86, 89, 148, 149, 180, 181

K

Kaaba 56
Kabballah 8, 14, 57, 86, 89, 131–134, 136, 138, 139, 141, 145, 146, 151, 152, 163, 178, 184, 190–193, 198, 212
Kavanot 212
Keruvim 212
Keter 153, 191, 212
King Bee, Queen Bee 4, 7, 89
Kingdom of Israel 63, 66, 73
Kingdom of Judah 73, 86
King Solomon 8, 63, 78, 90, 104, 179, 181
Kishufim 212
Klal Yisrael 212
Klipah 212
Klipot 144, 212
Knight Templar 8
Kodesh Ha Kedoshim 212
Kol Ha Tor 212
Kotel Ha Ma'aravi 212
Kudlah 213
Kundalini 213
Kush 213

L

Levels of Creation 190, 213
Libya 78
Lifestreams 54
Lost Tribes 61, 63, 64, 75, 90, 117, 178
Luz 112, 213

M

Magid 213
Makom 213
Malakh 213
Malchut 147, 213
Manasseh 63, 66, 68, 72
Mary Magdalene 9, 111, 114, 177
Mashiach 213
Mauritania 78
Mayim chayim 213
Mazal 213
Mazikin 213
Mem 20, 25, 31, 32, 46, 53, 57, 132, 133, 147
Merkava 151, 213
Messianic/End Times 76
Metatron 133, 137, 163, 190, 214
Midrash 134, 143, 147, 149, 213
Mind 4
Mishnah 104, 134, 147, 212, 213, 214
Mispar 213

Mitzvah 213
Montauk: Alien Connection 4
Morocco 9, 78
Movements 13, 44, 107
Mt. Moriah 9, 182, 212

N

Nachash 213
Nefilim 98, 99, 213
Nogah 51, 213
North Africa 78, 79

O

Ohr Ha Ganuz 213
Olam Ha Bah 213
Olam Ha Zeh 213
Old Testament 70, 75, 81, 86, 184
Order of Sion of Jerusalem 113
O'rlah 213
Ottoman Empire 79, 107, 110, 180
Oversoul 54

P

Pardes 213
Partzufim 145
Peniel 214
Portugal 78, 111–116
Programming 4
Prophecy 71, 214
Pseudepigrapha 214
Pshat 213, 214

Q

Qabalah 15
Qabalists 15, 16

R

Rav 151, 196, 214
Reality 4
Reincarnation 146, 152
Remez 214
Rothschilds 110
Ruach Ha Kodesh 214
Rus Vikings 8

S

Sabbateans 105, 106, 107, 109, 110
Samech 132
Sanctification 137
Sandalphon 190
Sar ha Panim 214
Sasson 214
Sefer 14, 190, 213, 214
Sefirot/Sephirot 19, 20, 25, 26, 27, 28, 30, 46, 50, 117, 131, 132, 136, 137, 139, 141, 145, 147, 152, 153, 154, 189–192
Segulot 214
Sekhelim Nivdalim 214
Self 4
Sepher Yetzirah 14, 15, 16
Serafom 214
Ses 133
Sha'ashu'a 141
Shadai 214
Shechinah 214
Shedim 214
Shroud of Turin 114, 115
Sicarii 101, 102, 103, 104
Simbatyon 61, 64
Simcha 214
Simultaneous Existences 13, 54
Sod 141, 213, 214
Soul-Personality 54, 146
Star of David 74, 162

T

Talmud 102, 134, 143, 149, 211, 214
Tefilah 214
Tefillin 214
Tehom 214
Teli 214
Templars 9, 63, 104, 111–115
Template of God-Mind 4, 7, 13, 72, 89, 111, 112, 114, 137, 162
Teshuva 214
Tfillim 56
Therapeuts 8
The Thomas Code 157, 184
Tikun Olam 214
Tohu 146, 153, 215
Torah 63, 75, 89, 132, 134, 137, 139, 141, 144, 147, 148, 149, 155, 178, 181, 192, 198, 212, 213, 215
Transcendence 137
Tree of Life 16, 17, 38, 117, 189, 211
Tribe of Dan 72

Tribe of Joseph 72
Tribe of Judah 72
True Reality 4
True Reality of Sexuality 4, 56
True World History 4, 95, 111
Tunisia 78
Tzedaka 215
Tzelem 215
Tzimtzum 13, 62, 141, 142, 146, 152, 153, 190, 191, 215

V

Viking Priests 9
Vikings 8, 96, 104, 115, 117, 119, 122, 124

W

West Bank 72
White Owl Legends 4

Y

Yagon 215
Yehoshua 141, 147, 178, 183
Yemen 78
Yerushalayim 215
Yeshiva 148, 215
Yeshua 143, 145, 147, 178, 183, 184, 185, 215
Yesod 137, 153, 190, 213, 215
YHVH 136, 141, 142, 145, 190, 198, 215

Z

Zion 64, 137, 215
Zohar 8, 86, 89, 98, 111, 131, 136, 139, 146, 151, 163, 178, 180, 189, 191, 192, 193, 198, 212, 215
Zugots 136